Building with Awareness

THE CONSTRUCTION OF A HYBRID HOME
DVD & GUIDEBOOK

Guidebook
Written, Photographed, and Designed by
Ted Owens

DVD Video
Written, Directed, Photographed, and Edited by
Ted Owens

Learn More and Watch a Video Clip At
www.BuildingWithAwareness.com

DVD and Guidebook Published by
Syncronos Design Incorporated
www.BuildingWithAwareness.com

Distributed by
New Society Publishers
www.NewSociety.com
1-800-567-6772

Building with Awareness

THE CONSTRUCTION OF A HYBRID HOME
DVD & GUIDEBOOK

For my parents,
Peggy and Al Owens,
for their inspiration and encouragement

Ted Owens

DVD Video Contents

1. **INTRODUCTION**
   Solar energy and the big picture

2 **DESIGN**
   Completed house walk-through
   Design and materials overview
   Solar energy and windows
   House plans
   Crew member introduction
   Workshop construction

3 **BREAKING GROUND**
   Preliminary work
   Concrete reduction
   Rubble trench foundation: drawing
   Foundation: construction
   Plumbing
   Interior adobe wall foundation forms
   Foundation: forms and rebar
   Foundation: pouring concrete
   Radiant floor heat
   Pouring the concrete floor

4 **RAINWATER CISTERN**
   Introduction to cisterns
   Construction

5 **ADOBE**
   Adobe wall construction
   Using speed leads
   Gringo blocks and anchor bolts
   Construction of bond beams

6 **FRAMING**
   Introduction to framing systems
   Post-and-beam construction
   Ceiling joists and loft floor
   Roof trusses
   Roof overhang construction
   North roof framing
   Roof sheeting

7 **STRAW BALE WALLS**
   Straw bale workshop introduction
   Notching bales for posts
   Anchoring bales to posts
   Vertical rebars within bales
   Trimming and filling
   Installing metal roof sheeting

8 **ELECTRICAL**
   Photovoltaic system
   Wiring the house
   Compact fluorescents

9 **WINDOWS AND INSULATION**
   Bamboo arches
   Wire mesh on walls
   Installing windows
   Wallboard for ceiling
   Cellulose insulation
   Well pump installation
   Stucco splash zone
   Final mud prep: window seats, etc.

10 **EARTH PLASTER**
   Mixing and application
   Application on adobe

11 **FINISH WORK**
   Reed wall
   Paint and shellac
   Acid-stained floors
   Raised floor
   Gypsum plaster
   Kitchen cabinets and tile

12 **FINISH EARTH PLASTER**
   Mixing white earth plasters
   Application of white earth plasters
   Final exterior earth plaster

13 **CONCLUSION**
   Finished home
   Production credits

DVD SPECIAL FEATURES
- Second audio track with additional design
  and building commentary. This track is
  accessible by choosing Audio 2 with your
  DVD remote control.
- Narrated slide show of construction details
- Video sequence on how to split a straw bale

TOTAL RUNNING TIME OF MAIN PROGRAM
  2 hours 42 minutes

TOTAL TIME OF ALL CONTENT
  Over 5 hours 45 minutes

Guidebook Contents

1. Introduction

The winds and the waves are always on the side of the ablest navigator.
Edward Gibbon
English Historian

Building with awareness is recognizing the pros and cons of each decision made during the design and construction of a home. Only when informed decisions are balanced against one another can the energy efficiency, durability, and aesthetics of a structure be expected to outperform the "common" building techniques in use today. There are many different ways to design and build a green home. There are various materials and techniques to choose from, none of which is perfect for every area or structure. What is needed is awareness of the options. Decisions can then be based on the best information at hand. This is counter to a common approach to home construction that a structure is built a specific way mainly because it has always been done that way.

This book is the companion to the *Building With Awareness* DVD video. Whereas the DVD covers both aesthetics and construction techniques, the book leans towards the nuts-and-bolts of construction. A future publication in the *Building With Awareness* series will deal with the philosophy and implementation of aesthetic and energy-efficient design.

The DVD follows the construction of one straw bale, solar home from start to finish. Since this is a case study of the building of an actual home, it was essential to decide on specific design parameters and construction techniques. This differs from many books on straw bale construction and green building that tend to show a wide variety of techniques. Both methods have assets. The advantage of following the building of a single home is learning the real-world reasons why specific decisions were made and how each step related to the next. It would have been possible, and viable, to have used a different set of construction parameters than the ones used in this home and also have had an equally successful building project.

The ideas presented here are not advocating that this is the best way, or the only way, to build a home. It is just the way we chose to proceed—based on our research, needs, available materials, local climate, local experts, state and national codes, and budget. Some building techniques were mandated by local code. Some were just personal preference. Your design and construction techniques will vary as well.

If you are new to home building, you may decide to have a contractor do some or all of the work. If you decide to build most of the house yourself, you will want to find people with the appropriate knowledge to help you. It is es-

By taking advantage of what nature offers, instead of rejecting it, the mechanical heating and cooling system can be greatly reduced in size or even eliminated.

sential to find skilled people in your community who are knowledgeable in the specific areas of your project. By doing this, you will make fewer mistakes, work faster, and learn more.

One advantage in documenting this home is that, as the designer/documenter, I have been able to see how certain decisions are holding up with time. Having lived in the house for a few years, I now have first-hand experience as to what worked well and what I would do differently with the next construction project. Many times I have asked an architect or builder how a specific material held up after a few years of use. The usual answer was that no one knew. The home was sold upon completion, and no follow-up was done with the occupants. This is unfortunate because it slows down innovation due to the lack of resultant information. It is often the mistakes made that provide the best learning experiences, without which progress is impeded. To quote Barry LePatner: *Good judgment comes from experience, and experience comes from bad judgment.*

Sustainable homes create a comfortable living environment, regardless of the weather outside.

One purpose of the DVD, and especially this book, is to point out the lessons we learned so that others might benefit from our education—just as this project was often based on the lessons learned from the projects of others. Every construction project is a series of decisions based on the best information which one has at the moment. It is also an interconnected series of procedures which arise from on-the-spot problem solving. This is what innovation and progress are all about. Every time we create, we strive to do something better. There is no destination, only a direction.

In summary, there is always more than one way to solve a problem when building a hybrid home. It is important to consider how all of the elements work together and influence each other. Whatever your design choices, know why you came to a particular design decision. We will all be building better green homes in the future based on what we learn today.

The completed home is small, simple, elegant, and energy-efficient. The visual style arises from the use of natural materials and not from a complex shape.

2. DESIGN

Hybrid structures are built using a wide variety of materials. The term "hybrid" is among a collection of many names used to indicate a different approach to building design. Sustainable design, green building, and energy-efficient design all move in the direction of doing more with less. Hybrid is a term that has evolved in the car industry as it combines older and newer technologies. An internal combustion engine, which is paired with an electric motor and battery, creates something more energy-and-cost-efficient than either element on its own. The hybrid aspects of this particular home use low-tech mud bricks and earth plaster to absorb heat and thus aid in both heating and cooling. High-technology photovoltaic panels on the roof convert sunlight into electricity without the need for moving parts or for the burning of fossil fuels.

The home was designed and built using both conventional and progressive building techniques and thus balances the best of both worlds by using what is most appropriate for each particular job. Despite the structure's small footprint of 800 square feet, each room feels spacious and bright. By building the home no larger than was needed, money could be put into aesthetic elements instead of square footage. Thus the utility bills for heating and cooling go down. Although the layout is very compact, these basic concepts can be scaled to a structure of any size.

Natural materials (materials that are mostly created by nature, such as mud, straw, bamboo, stone, and wood) have many advantages. They contain low-embodied energy, which is the amount of energy required to actually create the materials. Sunlight was the energy used for growing the straw, and the earth and clay were dug from the ground. Natural materials also tend to be non-toxic, and they lend themselves to the creation of aesthetically pleasing structures with a minimal amount of skill on the part of the home builder. In this home, the choice of materials was based on their visual appeal, ease of use, energy efficiency,

The straw bale wall with the window is coated with 1" of earth plaster and a finish coat of ¼" unpainted gypsum plaster. The rear wall is adobe which is finished in brown earth plaster. The section above the flagstone wainscotting has a skim-coat of white earth plaster on top of the brown-colored earth plaster. The floor is salvaged oak.

We shape our dwellings, and afterwards our dwellings shape us.
Winston Churchill

and the amount of embodied energy.

The materials and design parameters of a building will change, depending on the climate and region. This is also true for the aesthetic style of the structure. These factors must be taken into account when envisioning your own home, as the visual look of this project is not "the" style for straw bale or green building. The aesthetics presented here came from the region and the use of locally available materials.

For the sake of simplicity, the design can be broken down into two categories. First, there is the structural design. This consists of the physical structure itself and includes the materials, the engineering, and the actual position of the home in relation to the sun. The second category is the visual design—what the house looks like aesthetically.

In a conventionally built home, the structure and appearance are somewhat tied together. Usually the designer is able to proceed more freely since sun angles, room and window placement, and room function are frequently not connected to the ideology of energy efficiency.

In the past, solar homes could be unattractive because the problems of merging solar design with aesthetics were not properly addressed. This problem came to the public's attention in the 1970's when many individuals began to seriously experiment with solar home design. Appearance wise, the green building movement may have been set back by the perception that energy efficiency was synonymous with ugliness. Odd roof and ceiling angles, too many windows in one place and not enough in another, too many macramé-suspended hanging plants and free-form tree trunk beams, and little knowledge of how to balance appropriately these design elements led to houses that did not engender praise from the general public. Some called it the "hippie-look." The good intentions sometimes made it appear that the engineer and designer were not working in harmony. It is not uncommon for the aesthetics of a newly-designed object to suffer when the engineering is still in the early stages. Fortunately, this is not as often the case today. Being sustainable, energy efficient, and visually pleasing are all essential elements of good green design. One can give form to the other and can create beauty as a side benefit to enhancing the sustainable qualities of a home.

Top: All of the color in this room comes from the natural materials themselves, not from paint.

Left: The loft has a cozy tent-like feel. The deep window insets reflect soft light around the room and create a window shelf. According to code, if a loft is going to be used as a sleeping area, it is supposed to have a full-size staircase.

Below: In the entry hall, winter sunlight hits the adobe thermal mass wall to the left.

otice in the floor plan to the right that all of the exterior walls are constructed of straw bales. This will reduce the heat of the summer and the cold of the winter indoors. For the interior walls it is very important to get as much thermal mass (thick, heavy walls of a material such as adobe or stone) as possible within the outer shell of the highly insulating exterior walls. The thermal mass walls absorb heat as sunlight enters through the south-facing windows. The heat is released back into the room when the air temperature of the room drops below the temperature of the warm walls. The windows and the thermal mass both contribute to the passive solar heating and cooling. In the summer, the cooler thick walls absorb heat from the warm rooms, thus cooling them.

This home has extensive thermal mass, and all of the direct sunlight entering the building hits these heat-storing materials. In the winter, much of this sunlight is absorbed directly by the thermal mass walls. (See the floor plan to the right and the time lapse cinematography sequence within the DVD.) The remaining sunlight warms the 4-inch-thick concrete, thermal mass floor. It is not necessary that all sunlight hit a wall or floor directly, as the home is designed to reflect light (and therefore heat energy) throughout the room. Although direct sunlight does not quite reach the center 24"-thick thermal-mass wall, this wall does absorb reflected heat. On the other hand, it acts as a cooling element in the summer.

Keep in mind that this home, despite being in a high desert area where many summer days reach the upper 90's (°F), does not contain any mechanical air-conditioning system. Cooling of this home was considered a greater challenge than the heating—despite winter nights that can be in the mid-teens or lower. The inclusion of an air-conditioning system could have easily doubled the cost of the photovoltaic electrical system, so much attention was placed on thermal mass cooling. For about half of the year, the interior thermal mass is used exclusively for air cooling. Windows are opened at night to take advantage of the local climate's cool night air which will remove heat from the thermal mass. In the morning, the windows are closed, and the dense walls then absorb much of the day's heat that reaches the living space.

The room temperature in this home can remain at around 70° F even when the outdoor temperature peaks at 96°. If the average home built today could maintain a 26° temperature difference without mechanical cooling, the nation's summer electrical consumption would drop dramatically.

This home was an experiment in maximizing thermal mass. It would be difficult to add too much mass. That said, the 24" thick wall could be reduced to 14" or 10" (if using adobe) and still be very effective at heating and cooling while gaining more floor space at the same time. (See page 144 for more information.)

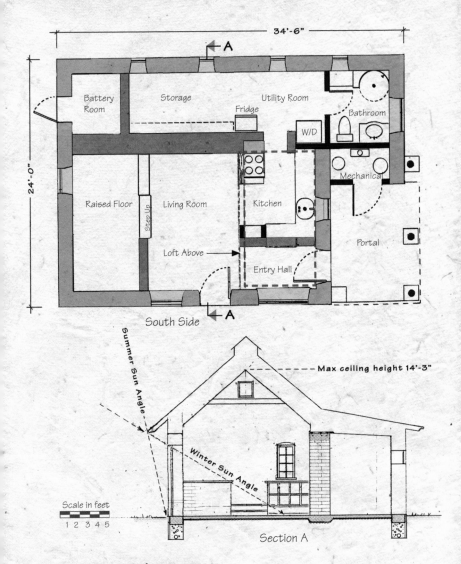

34'-6"

24'-0"

Battery Room

Storage

Utility Room

Fridge

Bathroom

W/D

Mechanical

Raised Floor

Step Up

Living Room

Kitchen

Loft Above

Portal

Entry Hall

South Side

A

A

Summer Sun Angle

Max ceiling height 14'-3"

Winter Sun Angle

Scale in feet

1 2 3 4 5

Section A

FLOOR PLAN AND ELEVATION

Total Square Footage (includes walls and loft)	832 square feet
Total Interior Square Footage *	647 square feet
Loft Square Footage (including side storage)	91 square feet
Angle of Roof and Photovoltaic Panels	40 degrees
Total Roof Area	1,064 square feet

Adobe

Straw Bale

Wood Frame

All measurments are approximate.
* Less exterior straw bale walls and mechanical room. Includes the loft.

Exterior Walls:
Insulation

The advantages of using straw bale are: it is a waste product; it is an excellent insulator (R-30 to R-40 when plastered and depending on the thickness of the bale); it makes very thick walls that are aesthetically pleasing. (See pages 90-101.)

straw

Interior Walls:
Thermal Mass

Instead of using conventional wood-frame walls and wallboard, it is best to have at least some thick and heavy walls that can absorb, hold, and release heat. This stabilizes the indoor temperatures, as the outdoor temperature may vary 40 degrees during the day. Depending on what is available in your area, the material might be adobe, rammed earth, stone, or brick. Concrete or cement block can also be used. However, they are less desirable due to the energy used and the pollution generated in the manufacturing process. Ideally, at least 1/2 to 2/3 of the interior surfaces (floor and walls) should be thermal mass. (See Concrete on page 29.)

stone

mud

4"

Left: If your budget limits the thickness of your thermal mass walls, strive for about 4" of solid wall thickness as this will give you good performance for your money. The indicated first 4" of the wall thickness is most effective at storing and releasing heat over a 24-hour period.

R-value: A measure of the capacity of a material, such as insulation, to impede heat flow, with increasing values indicating a greater ability to insulate. Straw bales are about R-1.45 per inch. Some products, such as windows, are rated in U-values. The U-value is a measure of thermal conductance (the amount of energy that will be lost) and is inversely related to the R-value. Here is the formula to convert one value to the other: U-value = 1 ÷ R value R=1 ÷ U value

The Workshop

Straw/clay
or cob infill

Bond beam

Adobe

Durable splash
guard

Upper Photo: The workshop was constructed before the home. It housed on its roof the photovoltaic electrical system that allowed us to build the home off the electric grid. This small structure also was a place to store tools and equipment. This is the view from the east side.
Lower Photo: This west view shows some of the materials that were used. Straw/clay has sufficient mud mixed with the straw to make it stick together (see the slide show on the DVD). Cob has more mud and is a denser material.

The Basics of Passive Solar Heating and Cooling

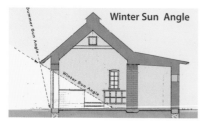

Winter Sun Angle

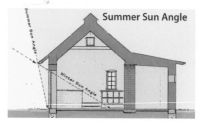

Summer Sun Angle

The sun is low on the horizon at high noon in winter. The roof overhang and windows allow sunlight to enter the home. When it strikes the darker-colored surfaces of the floor and walls, this light energy is converted into heat energy. The thermal mass absorbs this heat and slowly releases it back into the rooms at night.

The summer sun is high above the horizon at noon. The roof overhang now prevents direct sunlight from entering the home. This keeps the interior much cooler. You can actually design the overhang to cut out direct sunlight in the month that you choose. If your spring season is still cold, more sunlight can be allowed to enter.

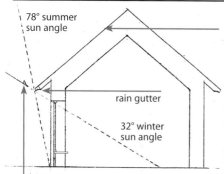

78° summer sun angle

rain gutter

32° winter sun angle

Sun Angles: Pay attention to the construction details when designing your roof overhangs. Rain gutters, window molding, and the distance the window is inset from the outside wall surface will all influence the amount of sunlight that can enter the home. Include these details in your cross-section drawing.

Draw the angles by using a protractor. It is easiest to draw the sun angles and the cross section on two separate sheets of tracing paper and then overlay the sun angles over the cross section. This permits fine-tuning the overhang distance.

The southern wall of the home can vary 15° or so from true south and still work very well.

Roof Slope: Since the photovoltaic panels are attached to the roof, the angle of the roof was determined by the most efficient slope for pointing the panels towards the sun. When winter electrical generation is the most important, the PV tilt angle should be set at the latitude angle plus about 15° degrees. To maximize summertime production, orient the PV tilt angle at latitude minus about 15° degrees. As an example, the latitude of Albuquerque, New Mexico, USA, is about 35° N. The roof angle of this home, and thus the angle of the PV panels, is 42°. This was a compromise setting between the ideal winter and summer angles.

Determing Your Sun Angle: The sun angle in the northern hemisphere at noon on the longest day of the year (June 21) and on the shortest day of the year (December 21) may be determined from the following simple equations:
June 21 noon sun angle = 113.5° minus the latitude
December 21 noon sun angle = 66.5° minus the latitude
Example: Albuquerque, NM latitude = 35° N
June 21 noon sun angle = 113.5°—35 = 78.5°

For more information on sun and PV angles, visit: **www.BuildingWithAwareness.com** and click on **References**

Window Placement

South Side

The long south side of the house contains most of the window area for the collection of solar energy (sunlight) in the winter months. In this case, the glass area is approximately 17% of the floor area. The roof overhang is properly designed to keep direct sunlight out of the home in the summer. The southern orientation of the home is based on using true north, as opposed to magnetic north.

West Side

Windows on this side are kept to a minimum and as small as possible to prevent overheating of the home in the late afternoon of summer. Planting a large shade tree on this side would also help. Large windows would have created the need for an air-conditioning system. This, in turn, would have required a dramatically larger photovoltaic system for power.

North Side

Windows on this side are just large enough to supply daylight to the interior and to supply cross ventilation in the summer. In the winter, large north windows will only drain money from your bank account and transfer it to the utility company.

East Side

Like on the west side, the east-side windows, if too large or unprotected, will allow the home to gain heat on summer mornings. The portal gives some protection from the sun. The loft window vents out warm air at night while cooler air enters the lower windows. The horizontal bathroom window is high enough for privacy yet still permits a view of the mountains.

Overview of Materials

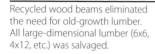

Recycled wood beams eliminated the need for old-growth lumber. All large-dimensional lumber (6x6, 4x12, etc.) was salvaged.

The southern side of the home collects solar energy for the purpose of heating and electrical power generation.

Fast-growing aspen wood is used for the kitchen ceiling/loft floor and was painted with a **non-VOC paint** to reflect light. (See page 82.)

Note the angled steps on the ladder to the loft. The ladder swings out when in use and the steps become parallel to the ground.

This is a straw bale wall with earth-plaster base coat and 1/4" finish coat of gypsum plaster with a clear sealant to protect from stains around the sink.

This adobe wall adds thermal mass, soft-divides the two living spaces, and adds shelf, counter, and sitting space.

The west wall of the living room has a skim coat of unpainted gypsum plaster. The lighter-colored walls help to distribute light and also add visual appeal. Since construction, there has been no cracking or separation of the materials.

The raised floor is surfaced with recycled oak. For protection it has a coat of **shellac** and wax. Panels in the floor lift up to gain access to additional storage below. (See page 129.)

Acid-stained concrete floors provide extra thermal mass for absorbing sunlight that enters through the south-facing windows. The 4"-thick floor also contains the backup hydronic radiant-floor heating tubes. (See page 45.)

Bamboo was used for the horizontal rungs of the loft railing.

Wood-frame cabinet has an earth-plaster finish on top. This transitions into an adobe thermal mass wall facing the south window.

The straw bale exterior wall features a three-coat earth plaster finish of 1-2". (See page 120.)

Cast-in-place concrete countertops sit atop simple wood-frame cabinets. The countertops absorb heat from the south-facing windows in the winter and add to the thermal mass. The cabinet doors were owner-built and feature bamboo within a wood frame.

Non-VOC paint: VOC stands for "volatile organic compounds." This is the solvent you smell in conventional house paints. Non-VOC paints are less polluting in the manufacturing process and while painting. This is a superior product----for the sake of the environment and the painter. Many of the major paint manufacturers now offer these products.

Shellac: A natural polymer secreted by the Lac insect. When mixed with alcohol, it becomes a natural varnish that can be painted on wood. Once dry, it is non-toxic (and even termed edible as it is sometimes used to coat pills).

B efore breaking ground, check with the building department of your city or town and see what permits will be needed and who is required to stamp your construction drawings (architect and/or structural engineer, etc). This can be a tedious and time-consuming process. There is a learning curve as to whom you will need to consult, what signatures you will need, and what fees will be due.

You will also want to see what is required in the way of sewage hookups or septic permits, as this will determine where your sewer pipes will run. In this town, all sewage is processed on-site using a septic system, so we had that installed early in the building project. This guaranteed that the 1/4" per foot slope of the sewer pipe from the house to the septic tank would mate at the proper height with the septic system's input pipe.

If you need an electrical hookup by the utility company, this will also have to be arranged. This home was built using power from our own photovoltaic electrical system. Until the system was installed in our as-yet-to-be built workshop, we used manual hand saws and charged our battery-powered drills elsewhere. A generator was rented for one day to run a power saw in order to build the roof trusses. If you do plan to build using your own sunlight-or-wind-generated electricity, these system components will have to be ordered ahead of time as well.

Straw bales were ordered to ensure that we had a supply when needed. Check with your bale supplier to see what months of the year they are stocked. It is a seasonal business, so plan ahead. The same is true for adobe. In New Mexico, the adobe yards shut down in the cold winter months. Now is also a good time to start looking for salvaged materials such as large-dimensional wood, sinks, wood for floors, etc. All of these materials take time to find; you will have to keep your eyes open for what may become available at the salvage yard.

A backhoe was contracted for earth moving and digging. It is a good idea to get at least two bids, as moving and compacting dirt can be expensive.

1   A first step is to roughly lay out the position of your home on the lot. This is just to get a feeling for where the structure will be situated. Use bamboo, string, or rocks for making the outline on the ground. This step is to make sure that there are no unforeseen problems before committing to an accurate placement. It will give you a final chance to ensure that your south-facing windows will not be blocked by the shadow of trees and that your views will be what you expect. Much of this should also have been considered when you were designing the home.

A transit-level is used to precisely locate the home on your land, as shown on your plans. Find one prominent corner and use this as your reference point for everything else. By using a rented transit-level and a good book on surveying for beginners, siting the position of a small home is fairly simple. This is a two-person job. Hiring a professional surveyor is another option, of course.

Locate and install the batter boards precisely by running a string from the structure's corner stakes to where the batter board will be located. Batter boards should be very stout, as they must withstand the abuse of construction through the foundation pour. Use either metal stakes, 2x3s, or 2x4s. A key require-ment is to place these batter boards as far away as possible (at least 6') from the actual corners of the building. Otherwise, they will be constantly in your way as you navigate wheelbarrows around the site and dig trenches for plumbing and conduits.

Stake from survey showing the corners of the structure

Batter boards located at least 6' away

Indicates top of foundation. The yellow lines indicate string positions showing the width of the foundation.

Precisely mark the vertical batter board stakes to indicate the height of the top of the foundation. This can be done with a water level (see page 37). The horizontal crosspiece is then attached at this height and becomes a precise indication of the finished foundation height. Horizontal pieces are added to show the location of the inside and outside edges of the foundation. At various times during construction, the strings will be removed for convenience. A permanent mark on the batter board will allow you to quickly and precisely reposition the string.

What is the environmental concern with concrete, and what can be done about it?

Portland cement is a miraculous building material. It is a powder that, when mixed with water, cures due to a chemical reaction. It literally becomes stone-like and even gains strength with age. When mixed with gravel and sand, it is called concrete and is much stronger than the cement alone. Concrete can be molded and formed into almost any shape. It is one of the basic construction components used throughout the world.

The production of portland cement generates approximately 7% of all greenhouse gasses on the planet—a fact not known to many people. Therefore, how and where this material was used in the building of this house received careful consideration. In some cases, it was not used at all but was replaced by a more sustainable alternative. In cases where concrete was appropriate, it was used judiciously to serve, whenever possible, the multiple purposes of structural need, aesthetic element, and thermal mass. Foundations can use a substantial amount of concrete, particularly when they are 18" wide, the width of a straw bale wall. A rubble trench foundation in this house reduced the amount of concrete by more than 50% as compared to a typical foundation.

There are ways to specify a much greener concrete mix. Coal fly ash is an abundant waste product from coal-fired electrical plants. Fly ash, if possible, should be added to pre-mixed concrete delivered ready to pour from a cement mixer truck. The more fly ash added to concrete, the less portland cement is needed. 15% to 20% fly ash is now commonly added to concrete in many areas. Not only is it a waste product that reduces the amount of portland cement and thus reduces greenhouse gasses, but it also improves the strength of the concrete and reduces the amount of water needed for the mix. You will need to check with your local concrete distributor and/or architect to see how much fly ash can be added for your particular project. Unfortunately, fly ash is not currently available in dry-mix bags of concrete and portland cement that are purchased at your local building supply store.

Transit-level: An instrument that is similar to a precision telescope with a bubble level. It permits the builder to site in both elevations and angles. A plumb bob hangs beneath the transit for precise positioning over a marker. An assistant holds a graduated measuring rod that aids in transferring the precise elevation from one point to another. Distances from point to point are measured with a measuring tape.

Batter boards: Reference markers placed outside of the corner stakes. This permits the corner stakes to be removed when the foundation trenches are dug. The batter boards consist of two vertical stakes connected with a horizontal crossbar.

Anatomy of a Rubble Trench Foundation

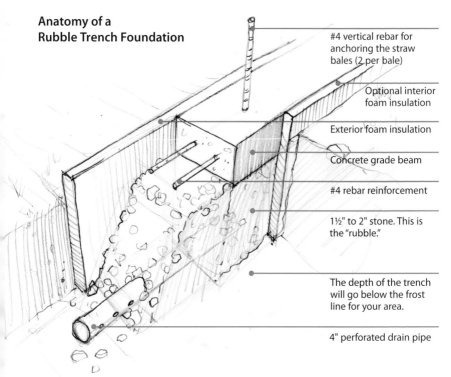

#4 vertical rebar for anchoring the straw bales (2 per bale)

Optional interior foam insulation

Exterior foam insulation

Concrete grade beam

#4 rebar reinforcement

1½" to 2" stone. This is the "rubble."

The depth of the trench will go below the frost line for your area.

4" perforated drain pipe

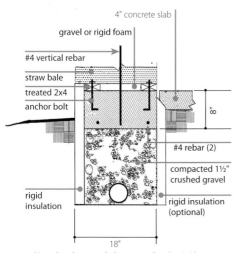

4" concrete slab

gravel or rigid foam

#4 vertical rebar

straw bale

treated 2x4

anchor bolt

8"

#4 rebar (2)

compacted 1½" crushed gravel

rigid insulation

rigid insulation (optional)

18"

Note that the straw bale can overlap the rigid foam insulation on the outside.

A rubble trench foundation replaces the majority of the concrete with broken stone. This foundation is as sturdy as a conventional foundation. The foam insulation reduces the loss of heat from the interior of the home, and it is required by code in many areas. The foam can be placed on either side or both sides of the trench. We placed it on the outside since the rubble itself is a bit of an insulator due to the air spaces between the gravel. It is likely that either an architect's or a structural engineer's stamp will be required on plans for a rubble trench foundation.

Left: This is an architectural drawing showing the use of wood for raising the straw off the floor level (see page 49). We used the method shown in the top drawing where the wood was replaced with concrete. Note the thermal break between the floor slab and the grade beam.

2 The foundation trenches are dug with a backhoe. In hindsight, because of the sandy soil that was on the site and the small footprint of the house, the trenches could have been dug by hand with a shovel. The soil was also free of rocks, which made digging quite easy. The problem with using a backhoe for a very small home is that the room to maneuver it is limited. The bucket was a bit wider than we needed, and this made for some extra work on the rubble trench foundation. If your soil is rocky, a backhoe is the only way to go.

3 After dampening the soil with a watering can or hose, a rented compactor is run over the bottom of the trenches. This ensures that the foundation will not settle over time and crack the walls of the home. Use diligence in ensuring that your home will stand the test of time. This will reinforce the image of the long-lasting quality that can be achieved by using these alternative building techniques.

4 The assembly of the actual rubble trench foundation can now begin. The perimeter drain, which runs around the entire perimeter of the foundation, is now laid. It consists of 4" diameter plastic perforated pipe and is glued together at all of the joints.

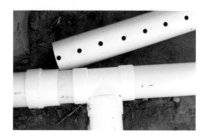

The holes are on the side of the pipe, so they do not show from this view. In years to come, any water that enters the foundation will drain out to a lower part of the yard. Although required by code, it is interesting to note that, since the pipe is open to a lower part of the property, the design could let water enter the foundation through the drain pipe if the surrounding lower area were to flood.

5 The foam used for foundations is closed-cell, moisture-resistant, and CFC-free. The insulation on this foundation is on the exterior only. Additional performance can be gained by adding the foam to the inside wall as well. Your local codes will tell you the R-value that is required. This foam, which is 2" thick, is serving both as insulation and as the form for the concrete grade beam. We found it easier to let the foam be higher than was actually needed. It was trimmed to the proper height at a later date, as indicated by the string guides from the batter boards.

1x2s are used to align the foam to the string guides. The string indicates the actual finished foundation height. The foam will ultimately be trimmed to this level.

6 As gravel is placed on the inside of the foam, dirt is placed on the outside at the same rate. This ensures that the foam does not bow in or out, and it keeps the insulation running in line with the string guide. If the trenches had been dug to the perfect width, the foam could have been affixed directly against the wall of the trench, thus eliminating the need for some of this backfilling with dirt. Thoroughly tamp down and compact the dirt and gravel.

7 The interior wall foundations for the adobe and frame walls are only 8" thick since they are not affected by the earth moving from freezing and thawing. Salvaged 1x8s were used for the forms, and 2x2 stakes support them. To save money, use salvaged wood, as the moisture in the concrete will damage the wood. The interior foundations are level with the floor. This foundation will support the adobe thermal-mass wall. Both the wall and foundation are the same width. We inadvertently dug our interior trenches a bit too deep, so we used some extra gravel from the work site to bring the height to the proper level. Gravel was actually not required, as the concrete could have been put directly on the dirt.

8 Two #4 rebars are installed within the forms. Steel support chairs are attached with wire to the rebar. The chairs ensure that the rebar will be suspended within the concrete and will not rest directly on the ground.

Plumbing and Buried Utilities

Plumbing and conduit for the utilities are installed concurrently with the foundation. This is called the drain, waste, and vent (DWV) plumbing, and much of it is located underneath the floor slab. Because of this, the work site can appear to be more trenches than level grade. In the small footprint of a compact house, this becomes even more evident as the pipe, conduit, and foundation trenches will all be exposed until the DWV plumbing is inspected by the building inspector. The trenches for conduit contain electrical wiring, telephone lines, and television and internet cable.

Two common materials are used to manufacture plastic drain pipe: PVC and ABS. Each of these materials poses serious environmental concerns, both in the manufacturing process and in disposing of the material at the end of its life cycle. Black ABS drain pipe appears to have fewer problems. PVC contains vinyl chloride, which is a known health risk to humans. In addition, when PVC burns, it produces hydrogen chloride gas as well as dioxins and chlorinated furans, all of which are extremely toxic. Although it is sometimes hard to do, PVC is a construction material to be avoided whenever possible. A greener alternative to plastic drain pipe would be cast iron pipe. This is much more expensive than plastic pipe, and installing it may be beyond the ability of the average do-it-yourselfer.

All of the fresh-water lines in this home are copper. PVC pipe is a very common material for these pipes as well. Although even copper has problems, it appears to be relatively safe unless your water is acidic. Copper, unlike PVC, can easily be recycled. There are also some interesting polyethylene potable-water plumbing systems coming on the market. Polyethylene may prove to be a greener alternative to either of the above.

For hot-water lines, use the narrowest pipe permitted by code. The narrower the pipe, the less water is wasted in flushing out the cold water in the line when the faucet is first turned on. The faster the hot water reaches the spigot, the less water goes down the drain and the less energy is needed to heat the water. A ½" inside-diameter pipe is more energy efficient than a ¾" pipe. It is important to keep the distance from the hot water source to the fixture as short as possible. This home has very short hot-water runs, as can be seen in the floor plan on page 19. All hot-water lines are insulated and run in the ceilings and frame walls.

Isometric perspective: A method of drawing that simulates perspective (objects appear to move away from the viewer) without the size of the object getting smaller as it recedes. In this case, all pipes conform to two different angles that always remain parallel to each other.

In order to obtain a permit to install our own plumbing, a simple schematic of the entire DWV system (see a detail of the drawing to the right) was submitted to the permit office. It was drawn in isometric perspective. The inspector's main concern will be that the DWV plumbing contains the proper size pipe for the water load and that there is proper venting to the roof. Check with your local building officials as to what plumbing you can install yourself and what permits are required. There are multiple books available on do-it-yourself plumbing.

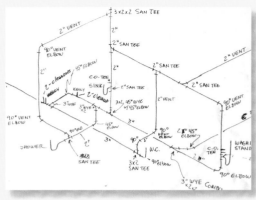

This is a temporary pipe that is about 10' in vertical height. All open pipe ends are capped throughout the waste-water system. The DWV plumbing is filled with water to the top of the vertical pipe. Any leaks are then easy to find.

Fresh water pipe from the well

Pipe to bathroom sink

Shower drain pipe

French drain for rubble-trench foundation

The gray-water pipe collects potentially reusable water from the shower, sinks, and clothes washer. Check with your local codes to see if any particular uses are prohibited.

Multiple exterior cleanouts—one for each direction of the pipe run

Black-water pipe from toilet and other fixtures that are not suitable for gray-water use

Renting a trenching machine will make digging much easier. If your work site is muddy, or if you have a lot of trenches to dig, spend the extra money to rent a trencher that you ride on. Following a rain, this hand-guided trencher became very difficult to maneuver in the mud.

Coiled 1" diameter copper pipe was used to bring water from the well to the home. Installation is simple as the pipe bends to your needs. Code will determine the depth based on the frost line in your area. When pipe extends through concrete, it must be wrapped with either pipe tape or foam so that the concrete doesn't contact the pipe.

Gray-Water Plumbing

Once the gray-water line is outside the perimeter of the house, the gray-water pipe passes through a diverter valve that permits this water to be channeled off to a future gray-water recycling system. At the time of construction, gray-water systems were not permitted in New Mexico. I assumed that the law would someday change, and it did. Now gray-water systems are permitted in the state. Hooking up the system will be quite simple here because all of the valves are already in place. By having an accessible diverter valve, the gray water can be made to flow back to the septic system when desired. Once past the diverter valves, both the black-water and gray-water lines merge into one and then proceed to the septic or sewer system.

This is a diverter valve for the gray water system. A second valve will be placed on the other line as well.

Draw a Map

It is very important to make detailed drawings, such as the one shown to the right, of everything that is buried. Include the distance from known landmarks, such as corners of the building, and the approximate depth of the pipe or conduit. This drawing will be placed in a notebook that will always stay with the home and will be passed on from owner to owner. The value of these drawings will be priceless to you in the future as you dig around the yard in landscaping or making repairs.

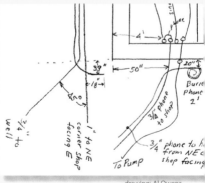

drawing: Al Owens

When one piece of rebar connects to the next section, the two pieces are overlapped and wired together. Note that the rebar overlaps and crosses from the inside to the outside at corners. This adds additional strength. When one of the foundations intersects another, the rebar also crosses from one side to the other. Rebar is bent with an inexpensive tool that is available from home supply centers.

9 A pre-marked master reference stake indicates the finished foundation height, and a water level is used to transfer this height to all parts of the foundation foam. This single stake becomes a guide for both the floor height and the foundation height. The floor height is two inches lower than the exterior foundation height since the foundation is raised to protect the straw bales.

DVD Location: 27 minutes 34 seconds

Left: A master survey stake with a reference mark showing the top elevation of the foundation
Right: The same elevation is transferred to the foundation foam. The two marks will be at the same height. This water level is a commercially available unit that has caps on the ends so that the water does not spill while being carried.

Water level: A simple device that is nothing more than a long tube filled with water. Due to gravity, water at one end of the tube will be at the same height as it is at the other end. One end is placed at a reference mark, and the other end can then be moved around the construction site, marking the same elevation where needed.

10 The positions of the J-bolts for the post-and-beam supports are marked on the foam forms. To conserve wood, straw bales are used for the inside of the concrete forms. Either vertical metal stakes or adobe bricks are used to keep the bales in place. Tar paper is then attached to the bales with nails so that the concrete will not bond to the straw. Adobes, or other bricks, can be used to reinforce the foam as well.

#4 rebar is hammered into the stone rubble. The rebar will extend vertically through one-and-a-half bales of straw (about 21" above the top of the concrete) for the finished wall. Since there are two rebars in each bale, it is necessary to know the position of each bale. This is simple to do if you designed the lengths of your walls on multiples of 36" for a full bale, or 18" for a half bale. Aluminum cans are used atop the rebar to avoid injury. Broad-headed plastic rebar caps are the superior choice for safety. See page 96 for alternatives to using rebar within the straw bale.

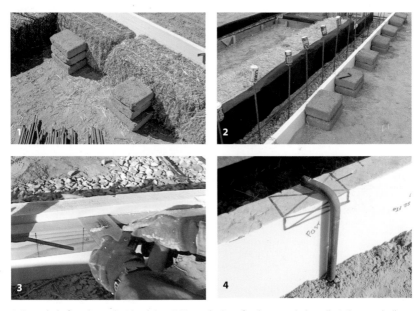

1. Straw bale form braced with adobes **2.** Vertical rebars for the straw bale walls **3.** Snap a chalk line to connect the elevation marks on the foam. 2x4s are clamped to the foam to act as a guide while cutting with a hand saw. **4.** Then mark the top of the foam to show the position of all of the vertical posts for the wall framing. The marks must be positioned precisely from your construction drawings as they are spaced for specific window and door sizes.

This corner area includes plumbing. This section was therefore framed with wood. The tops of the wood and the foam are at the finished foundation height, so leveling of the concrete is very simple.

11 Cross bracing is used to keep the framing of the home from racking (leaning to one side). There are many ways to add cross bracing to the structure. We chose to use metal straps (see page 101). To anchor the straps to the foundation, a metal J-bolt is imbedded in the concrete. A hole is drilled in the foam insulation, and the bolt is inserted with the threaded side extending out from the exterior wall. The J part of the bolt will be embedded within the foundation concrete. Check with your code officials or architect to determine what is best for your home.

Left: The J-bolt as seen from inside the concrete foundation form. This part of the bolt will be buried in concrete. The threaded end of the bolt will extend outside of the foundation foam.
Right: The completed wall with cross bracing straps. (See page 101 for the final assembly of the cross bracing.)

Lowering the foundation at every door is a very important step. Since the foundation is poured 2" higher than the finished floor level, the height must be dropped 2" at door openings. Scrap wood is used to form a dam so the higher concrete will not settle into the floor area. Remember that this area will be a visible floor area so it is important to finish it to the desired appearance.

DVD Location: 0 hours 32 minutes 17 seconds

12 Compute the volume of the concrete (in cubic yards: length x width x height) that will be needed to fill the area of the grade beam. You can then arrange for the delivery of the proper amount of premixed concrete. When the truck arrives, you must be fully prepared. Have at least one experienced crew member to coordinate the pour. This crew consisted of four workers. For a faster pour, make sure the shoot on the truck can reach most of your foundation area. Where it can't, a wheelbarrow can be used to distribute the concrete.

13 The concrete is screeded (leveled) to the proper height using a long board. By placing a carpentry level on the board, the concrete can be leveled flat even if one side of the form is straw bale and therefore not at the proper height. The interior wall forms are easier to screed since the forms themselves are at the proper height.

This is followed by using a trowel for the final finishing of the concrete. It should be reasonably smooth, although perfection is not required.

14 Anchor bolts are now inserted into the wet concrete. The bolt will have to be wiggled in to break through the gravel aggregate. It is then rotated so that the end of the J points away from the outside foam insulation. A string is run as a guide to position the bolts in a straight line and at the proper distance from the inside of the foam. Making sure that your bolts are in a straight line will ensure that your vertical wall posts and the beam will also be in a straight line.

15 Cover the entire foundation with plastic. The longer the concrete stays moist, the slower it sets, and the stronger it becomes. If you can, leave it covered for a week. If you pour your foundation when temperatures at night go below freezing, cover the foundation with tarps or straw bales to retain heat and prevent freezing. Ideally, allow five or six days before stripping the forms from the foundation.

The Concrete Floor

The floor of the entire house is exposed concrete that has been acid-stained to a stone-like patina. Since the use of concrete should be minimized because of environmental considerations, careful thought was given to the pros and cons of various types of flooring. Some of the choices considered were: a concrete floor with excellent thermal mass properties that would also be a good conductor of heat from the embedded hydronic heating system (a backup heating system is required by code); an earthen floor that has very low-embodied energy; a brick-on-sand floor with the radiant heating in a sand base below the bricks; flagstone with a concrete or sand base; or a wood or carpeted floor.

Wood flooring and carpet were out of the question due to the lack of thermal mass. Carpets wear out and thus create a disposal problem and long-term costs. Brick-on-sand would compromise the transmission of heat from the heating tubes to the dry sand and then to the bricks. Brick-on-concrete would work but would still involve the use of some concrete in addition to the brick. Flagstone had the same problem as the brick-on-sand and, in my opinion, is a bit more challenging to seal in an environmentally sound and aesthetic manner. An earthen floor would be a great alternative. However, due to the small footprint of the home and with 80% of the floor area being high traffic/high wear, this could have become a greater maintenance problem. An earthen floor, with the addition of aggregate, can perform quite well as a thermal mass. Many individuals, however, are not receptive to earth as an alternative flooring.

In conclusion, concrete was chosen because it is commonly used as a hidden base under a wide variety of finished floors. It also provides a great thermal mass, is visually pleasing, is easily maintained, and will not wear out, thus eliminating replacement surface materials for the life of the building. The downside is that it is higher in embodied energy. Looking at the overall energy efficiency of the building, I selected this choice as it followed our rule that, if concrete was used, it had to provide thermal mass, good aesthetics, extreme durability, and structural integrity. You may come to a different conclusion based on your needs. By adding 10-25% fly ash to the mix (see page 29), the concrete becomes more environmentally sound. The important point is to look at all of the options, with their pros and cons, and then to make a decision based on your best judgement. I definitely would have used earthen floors in low-traffic areas if the home were to have multiple bedrooms and closets.

There are more environmentally sound alternatives to the acid staining of concrete. In hindsight, I would have used an iron-based wash (the iron component that is used as an agricultural additive to soil) or would have added integral color to the concrete mix (although I rarely consider this choice the most aesthetic). That said, it is hard to beat the depth of color and beauty of an acid-stained concrete floor. (See page 128 for more information on this subject.)

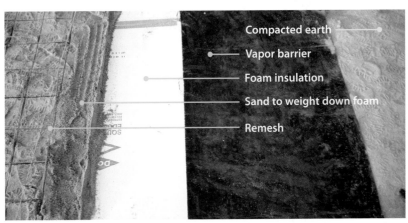

Compacted earth
Vapor barrier
Foam insulation
Sand to weight down foam
Remesh

The layers beneath the concrete floor.

1 Within the confines of the inner perimeter of the foundation, the earth is brought to the proper level to allow for a 4" concrete slab, foam, and sand. The base dirt should be thoroughly compacted to prevent settling.

Next, a vapor barrier is installed. This prevents moisture from wicking up into the floor. The 1" of foam insulation is installed to insulate the slab from the earth below. Holes are cut into the foam for plumbing and conduit.

About 2" of sand are added on top of the foam to keep it from blowing away.

Remesh is rolled out and cut to fit using heavy gauge wire cutters or a bolt cutter. The remesh reinforces the concrete slab and is used as an anchor for radiant floor tubing. When the concrete is poured, the remesh is pulled up a little to center it within the 4" slab. Steel support chairs should not be used here since they would only sink into the sand and foam when walked on during the installation process.

This floor will require 6-7" of height for the foam, sand, and concrete slab. Reference strings are run from the top of the foundation to act as a measuring guide. Remember that the foundation height for the exterior straw bale walls is about 2" above the finished floor level. The interior foundations are level with the floors. A 2x4 can be used to screed the dirt to the proper level.

2 A backup heating system for this home is required by code. Tubes of circulating hot water (heated by natural gas) place the heat where you feel it most—at your feet. This type of system is also quiet and does not dry out the air or stir up dust. The tubing is affixed to the remesh with twist ties. A continuous length of tubing starts at the mechanical room, loops around the floor, and then returns to the mechanical room for reheating. Your local supplier of radiant-heating equipment should be able to help you determine the size of your zones (the sections of the home that will be controlled by separate thermostats) and the spacing of the tubing. Although not difficult to install, local codes may require that the radiant tubing be installed by a contractor.

Left: Twist ties can be quickly tightened using this simple tool. This same tool is used for securing rebar to steel chair supports.

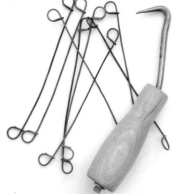

Copper header

Attaches to tubing with a compression fitting

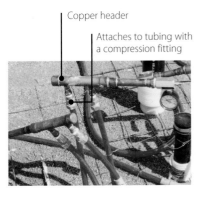

3 When all of the tubing is in place, the ends are connected to a copper header. All open ends are capped, a pressure valve is installed in each zone, and the line is pressurized with air using a hand pump or compressor.

The pressure valve will remain in place through much of the construction process (walls, framing, etc.). If you lose pressure, the source of the leak must be found and corrected.

4 The fast and efficient method of installing the floor slab is to have the cement delivered pre-mixed. A continuous monolithic slab is then poured. You can either do this yourself or hire a professional crew. The crew floats the concrete to a level surface. It is then troweled to a smooth surface and scored with grooves (control joints) to prevent cracking. If you have never poured a slab before, it is best to practice on a small pour first or, better yet, have someone on your crew who has experience.

The method we chose to create the floor was quite labor intensive. Our more artistic free-form floor required that we have additional time to score and manipulate the concrete into the desired organic patterns. This required pouring the floor in small sections so that there was time before the concrete set.

A conventional pour from a cement truck results in a monolithic slab. A float, which is like a large trowel on the end of a long pole, is used for the initial smoothing of the concrete. As the concrete stiffens, conventional hand trowels are used for the final finish.

A rented cement mixer is used to mix concrete by combining dry portland cement, gravel, sand, and water. This larger size two-sack mixer permitted the mixing of larger batches.

The concrete is transported by wheelbarrow to the area of the pour. Since the red radiant-floor tubing is resistant to tight bends, it passes through gray plastic 90° elbows to bring the tubing above the concrete in the mechanical room. Also note that the sewer pipe is covered with a thin white foam expansion joint where it penetrates the concrete floor. We used a crew of three people for creating the floor. Two would mix, pour, and do preliminary smoothing of the concrete. One would create the scored pattern and final troweling. The challenge is to pour and smooth the concrete, sketch the design into the wet cement with a stick, score the deep lines, and finish trowel the cement—all before the concrete sets.

5 The concrete is screeded (leveled) using a 2x4 board and a level. The board is moved back and forth along its length as it is dragged toward you to create a level surface. Low areas are filled with additional concrete. The right side of the board is resting on the interior foundation surface which is at the same level as the finished floor will be.

6 A wooden trowel is used for the preliminary smoothing of the concrete, resulting in a textured surface. This process is followed using a metal trowel that smooths the surface to the desired finish.

6 Sketching the pattern lightly into the concrete is best done while standing and using a long bamboo stick. At standing height, you can better see how your patterns relate to each other. This is an intuitive process, and at times I would erase my marks and start over.

7 The pattern is now worked into the wet concrete using a variety of tools. This is a back-and-forth process which includes working the joints and smoothing the surface with a metal trowel.

Section by section, the work continues. The foreground is partially scored. The section at the top is just being poured and screeded. The scores are up to 1/2" in depth and will be grouted as one of the final steps in building the home.

It was not my intent to try to simulate the look of a stone floor. The patterns were intended to be a bit more geometric. Since we ended up pouring during a spring heat wave, the patterns became a bit organic in appearance as we raced to smooth the concrete before it set.

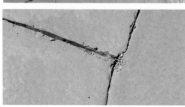

These are some of the tools used to create the seams within the wet concrete.

When stopping work for the day, the concrete is covered with plastic to hold in the moisture for a stronger and slower cure. Unlike the more typical monolithic pour from a concrete mixer truck, this surface is not perfectly flat and has more of the texture of stone. The entire floor is then covered with plastic for about a week.

Once the plastic is removed, the finished work is viewed in its entirety. The plumbing stubs and the wall anchor bolts mark the location of the interior walls. Note the circular shower area in the upper left hand corner. This was poured first with the perimeter about 1/4" lower than the surrounding floor. The shower floor then slopes ¼" per foot toward the drain. This helps to to keep the water within the shower area.

Using and Choosing Treated Wood For Foundations

4x4 post

Foam insulation infill

Embedded rebar

Treated 2x4

Side of concrete foundation

Anchor bolt with nut & washer

Whenever wood comes in direct contact with either earth or a concrete foundation, it must be treated to resist rot and termites. It is common in straw bale construction to raise the bales off the floor for flood protection by using pressure treated 2x4s with either insulating foam (shown above) or pea gravel as an infill. We chose not to go this route and raised the height of the concrete foundation instead. This was done to conserve wood and, more importantly, to stay away from wood treated with chromated copper arsenate (CCA), the most common wood preservative used. In 2004,

CCA was banned for use where human contact is possible (such as in decks and playground equipment) due to the toxic nature of the substance. Even though human contact would not be possible within the wall, it is still undesirable to have it in the home and to have the sawdust and scrap from the wood to contend with. The more healthful alternative to copper-based preservatives is wood treated with borate. Recycled plastic wood (made from recycled plastic bottles) is also a good alternative if permitted for your intended use.

4. RAINWATER CISTERN

Rain! whose soft architectural hands have power to cut stones, and chisel to shapes of grandeur the very mountains.
~Henry Ward Beecher

When the sun is out, the photovoltaic panels on the roof are generating electricity for the home. When it rains, the roof is collecting rainwater for the cistern. Metal and non-porous tile roofs are best. Wood shingles and asphalt-based roofs should be avoided, as they can contaminate the water. When properly collected, this resource is clean distilled water that is naturally soft. The use of rainwater does not cause iron and hard-water stains on fixtures. It also reduces the consumption of city and well water, both of which are becoming in shorter supply in many areas. In the case of this home, the rainwater is used for flushing the toilet, for the cold water in the washing machine, and for a gardening spigot. With an FDA-approved tank and appropriate filtering, a cistern can be used for supplying all of the water in the house. The cistern system demonstrated here uses readily available materials. Some cistern components, such as roof washers, are commercially available. We chose to make our own.

Rainwater from the downspouts passes through a wire screen to remove debris. It then fills up a roof washer that discards the first few gallons of water that come off the roof. The remaining cleaner water passes through a simple sand filter that removes dirt and sediment. Once filtered, the rainwater is transported by gravity through a pipe to the cistern, where it is stored until needed. As long as organic material is kept out of the tank (leaves, bugs, etc.), the water will remain usable for months. A small pump is used to transport the rainwater into the home via a separate plumbing system. This pump can be either a submersible type and underwater, or it can be outside the cistern, as is described in this chapter.

In our setup, the pump is used in conjunction with a pressure tank, which permits the water pressure to remain high for short periods of use before the pump turns on. The pump is able to pre-pressurize the tank to a higher pressure than the pump itself can maintain when it is running continuously. Depending on your needs and the type of pump used, the system can also be constructed without a pressure tank.

The size of the cistern tank depends on your water needs, the number of people in your home, the roof area of the structure, and how much rain you receive in your area. With a 1½-gallon low-flush toilet and a resource-efficient, front-loading washing machine, this 1,500 gallon tank, when full, supplies this home with non-potable water for up to four months without rain (does not include water for gardening).

Roof washer: A device which automatically removes and discards the first few gallons of rainwater that comes off the roof. This water is the dirtiest, as it contains dust and debris. Once the initial water is removed, the rest of the water goes directly into the cistern.

Buried electrical cable for the pump

The overflow pipe empties to a lower part of the yard.

Buried 50-gallon drum

Electrical outlet for the pump

A buried 50-gallon recycled drum houses the pressure tank and pump. Burying the system makes it less susceptible to freezing and also assists in keeping the pump below the water level of the tank, which aids in pumping efficiency. Flexible tubing is used from the drum wall to the pump, which permits lifting the pump/pressure tank assembly out of the drum without having to disconnect the water lines. Drainage holes are drilled into the bottom of the drum. The drum sits upon gravel that acts as a French drain. This will keep water away from the pump if there is ever a leak.

A riser with a twist-off lid allows the top of the tank to be buried about18 inches below ground. This protects it from freezing in the winter and keeps the water cool in the summer.

ABS drainpipe takes the rainwater to the cistern. The greater the square footage of the roof surface area, the larger the diameter of the pipe must be. For this home, the largest pipe is 4 inches in diameter.

A 1,500-gallon polyethylene septic tank is used as a cistern.

The pump pickup line is a flexible plastic pipe that has 2 separate parts. The first section goes from the pump to the threaded adapter on the outside of the tank. The second section is threaded to the adapter inside the tank and then goes below the water level of the tank.

2 hose clamps per connection are used to securely affix the tubing to fittings and the pump. The clear tubing is more flexible than the stiffer black tubing that is buried.

What we used

This 1,500-gallon polyethylene septic tank is easy to obtain and is reasonably priced at about 50 cents per gallon of capacity. If more capacity is needed, a larger tank can be obtained, or two or more tanks can be plumbed together. Some buried plastic tanks should not be allowed to go dry because of the possibility of the tank walls collapsing inward from the pressure of the surrounding earth. For this system, internal bracing was added to strengthen the tank.

Other Cistern Options

- Steel tanks with an epoxy coating to prevent rust
- Galvanized steel tanks for above-ground cisterns
- Fiberglass tanks
- Ferrocement tanks (thin-shell concrete)
- Concrete septic tanks
- Above ground swimming pools. These are the most cost effective, although not aesthetically pleasing. For safety, they must be covered to keep out debris, insects, animals, and people.
- Small, commercially available plastic cisterns used at each downspout
- 50-gallon, recycled storage drums placed at each downspout

What happens when the cistern goes dry during a severe drought?

Water can be added from a garden hose from the city-supplied water or from your well. If you do not have an adequate water supply, a water truck could be hired to fill the tank.

Tips

When using an external pump, keep the pump as low as possible relative to the bottom of the cistern. This will allow the pump to work more efficiently when the water level in the cistern gets low. The pump used in our setup is self-priming up to 12 feet above the tank water level, although we buried it for efficiency purposes as noted above. Another option would be to use a submersible pump at the end of the pickup line inside the cistern.

if your pump and pressure tank are outdoors, you may need to insulate the housing in order to prevent freezing in the winter. In this area a 2-inch-thick foam lid was cut from a piece of rigid foam insulation. A heavy piece of flagstone acts as a durable, attractive, and protective lid covering the foam beneath (see DVD).

1 A hole is dug to the proper depth for the tank. A backhoe was hired for this step. Screed (make level) the bottom of the hole with long boards and a level to ensure that you have a flat and compacted support surface. The bottom of the tank needs to be completely in contact with the bottom of the hole. Use care to ensure that the sides of the hole are secure and will not collapse.

2 The backhoe is used to push the tank into the hole. Note the use of a straw bale to protect the side of the tank from damage as it is being pushed. Two or three people could also push the cistern into place. If needed, 2x6s can be positioned in the hole as a ramp to ease the cistern to the bottom, or one side of the hole could be beveled as a ramp. With the tank in position, dirt is compacted around the base to fill in the voids.

3 The next step is to drill and plumb the cistern. One advantage of polyethylene tanks is that they are easily drilled into with a holesaw bit on your electric drill. It is best to attach pipes on the flat surfaces of the tank, as this will allow a better watertight seal.

This through-the-tank-wall compression fitting (second photo) features a rubber gasket and female threads for attaching the inside and outside pickup lines. Preventing air leaks is essential on the pickup line. Otherwise air will get into the line, the prime will be lost, and the pump will not be able to draw water.

A flexible pickup line is screwed into this fitting on the inside of the tank and should be long enough to permit pulling the pickup end out of the tank for servicing.

The end of the pickup line is fitted with a brass foot valve that prevents water from draining out of the line when the pump is off. A weight is used to keep the end of the pickup line positioned one or two inches above the bottom of the tank. This avoids drawing up sediment. Another option is to have the end of the pickup line on a float so that it draws water just a few inches below the surface, where it is the cleanest.

Brass Foot Valve

The drain line from the rain gutters passes through the wall of the tank by way of a simple homemade fitting constructed from two ABS pipe couplings—one inside and one outside of the tank. A short segment of pipe is cemented between the two couplings. While the cement is still wet, the couplings are pressed together against the wall from both sides. Silicone caulk is used to seal the junction against the tank wall, thus making it leakproof.

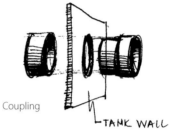

Coupling

└ TANK WALL

4 Trenches were dug for installing the drain pipe. To the right is the main water in line. ABS plastic sewer pipe was used for all drain lines. The main drain line that enters from the left is 4 inches in diameter since it is collecting water from several different downspouts on the house (with a roof collection area of around 1,000 square feet). The diameter of the pipe, or the number of pipes, may increase with a larger roof area. The line on the right is coming from the filter system serving the workshop roof. Since this carries a minimal amount of water, it is only 2 inches in diameter. The two lines

Coupling: a manufactured pipe fitting used to connect two pieces of pipe together. The coupling is of a wider diameter than the pipe itself, thus allowing it to slide over the pipe.

are connected by a wye. Note that there is a reducer fitting from the 4" pipe to the 2" pipe on the elbow. Remember that the supply pipe must have a 1/8" to 1/4" (or greater) slope per foot in order to ensure that the water flows downhill to the tank. With a 1/4" per foot drop, your pipe will be 12 1/2" lower at the end of a 50' run. Also keep in mind that your pipe must connect to the cistern above the highest possible water level of the tank. The greater the slope (up to 1/2" per foot), the more water can be run through a smaller diameter pipe.

TIP When burying any pipe or conduit, place a brightly colored plastic ribbon (available at home-supply stores) in the trench a few inches below the surface of the ground. This will help prevent you from cutting through the pipe with a pickax while landscaping or digging at a later date.

How many gallons of rainwater will you receive per inch of rainfall?

Formula: Projected roof area (bird's-eye view of the roof area in square feet) x 7.48 gallons per cubic foot ÷ 12 inches per foot

Example: How many gallons of water will be collected from 1 inch of rain on a 1,000 sq. ft. roof? (bird's-eye view)

1000 x 7.48 ÷ 12 = 623 gallons

Keep in mind that this is the amount received, assuming there is no water loss along the way. Leaky rain gutters and sand filters that are too small for the roof area (and therefore prone to overflowing) will reduce the amount of collected water.

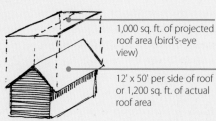

1,000 sq. ft. of projected roof area (bird's-eye view)

12' x 50' per side of roof or 1,200 sq. ft. of actual roof area

5 The interior bracing is a system that we devised. It works very well for the soil and freeze-thaw conditions that exist at the location of this home. Its suitability for all areas, conditions, and tanks cannot be guaranteed.

Interior cross braces are constructed of ABS plastic pipe and prevent the tank sides from bowing inwards when the tank is empty. Three of these cross braces were assembled and spaced evenly across the length of the tank.

#4 rebar is held within the 45-degree single wye by packing the pipe with portland cement. The rebar extends into the pipe for about 4". The outer end of the rebar is bent downward and fits into the milk carton.

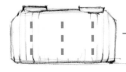

Side view showing cross brace positions.

The septic tank included a baffle that was left in place. The baffle divides the tank into two chambers. The drain line enters the smaller chamber. Sediment tends to settle in this side. The water pickup line is in the larger chamber of the tank that is relatively free of sediment.

The final assembly of the cross brace is done within the tank so that everything will fit through the tank access hatch. One-quart plastic milk jugs are used as pads where the brace contacts the tank. When filled with portland cement, the jug conforms to the side of the tank.

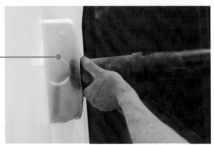

ABS 2" plastic pipe. Cut and dry fit all pieces outside of the tank. All plastic parts can be assembled with pipe cement made for ABS pipe or can be glued with silicone caulk for easier disassembly if needed.

SCH 40 ASTM-628-93 SOEX ABS CELLULAR CORE DWV [illegible] JOYCT ¼ 2"

45-degree double wye fitting

When everything is in place, the tank is buried. As dirt is added around the outside, a water truck is used to fill the tank to keep the water at the same level as the dirt. This balances the inward force of the dirt against the outward force of the water and keeps the tank walls from distorting. The side benefit is that you now have a source of water on the work site without having to wait for the first rain.

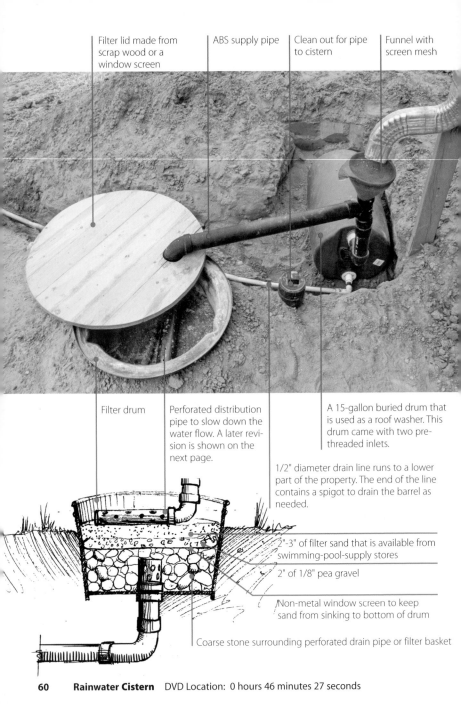

Filter lid made from scrap wood or a window screen

ABS supply pipe

Clean out for pipe to cistern

Funnel with screen mesh

Filter drum

Perforated distribution pipe to slow down the water flow. A later revision is shown on the next page.

A 15-gallon buried drum that is used as a roof washer. This drum came with two pre-threaded inlets.

1/2" diameter drain line runs to a lower part of the property. The end of the line contains a spigot to drain the barrel as needed.

2"-3" of filter sand that is available from swimming-pool-supply stores

2" of 1/8" pea gravel

Non-metal window screen to keep sand from sinking to bottom of drum

Coarse stone surrounding perforated drain pipe or filter basket

6 The filters, pumps, and pump-side plumbing are now installed. The simple filter system starts with a funnel which is covered with window-screen mesh to remove leaves and larger debris. The water will fill the roof washer, which is a buried drum or bucket. If not available locally, do an internet search for "15-gallon water barrels." Use a smaller drum if less volume is needed. The first water off the roof is the dirtiest, and this water fills up the barrel. The remaining, cleaner water backflows up the pipe into the sand filter. A handy filter container is a 24" galvanized metal drum, which is capable of handling about 1" of rain per hour from 530 square feet of roof area. The perforated distribution pipe slows down the water and distributes it evenly across the filter sand.

Downspouts should be positioned at least every 50 linear feet.

1. A hole is cut in the bottom of the metal drum, using a 2" holesaw bit for 2" pipe.
2. A screw-in fitting for electrical conduit is used to affix the ABS plastic pipe to the bottom of the drum. **3.** The threaded fitting will use 2 retainer nuts—one for each side--- to sandwich the fitting to the drum. **4.** The installed fitting is shown from inside the drum. Coat both the top and bottom retainer nuts with silicone caulk to make a watertight seal. **5.** A 90° long sweep elbow connects the drum to the drain pipe. Affix the elbow to the drum assembly with caulk in order to permit disassembly for later maintenance. **6.** The completed filter is shown before the addition of gravel and sand. A filter basket from a pool supply store prevents gravel from going down the drain.

Pump and Pressure Tank Assembly

Alternative Mount for Pump
This is an alternative location on which to mount the pump. We placed our pump below the tank for better efficiency and freeze protection.

Pressure Tank
This stores water under pressure so that the pump does not turn on every time a water fixture is turned on. A fitting on the bottom of the tank connects to the output-side of the pump. As the tank fills with water, the water pressure increases to around 45psi. This provides sufficient pressure for the cistern plumbing system.

Pressure Pump
Wire the pump according to the electrical code and pump specifications.

7. Large gravel is added and is followed by pea gravel, fine-mesh screen (to keep the sand from migrating downwards), and then swimming pool filter sand. **8.** A wire screen is added to the top of the drum to keep out bugs and animals. **9.** A close-up view of the 2″ diameter water spout. This section of ABS pipe has a cap on the end. Multiple holes are drilled in the pipe to distribute the water evenly and gently onto the sand. If needed, a small piece of flagstone can be placed on the sand in the area where the water flow hits it. Unlike the pipe shown in the filter on page 60, this one is suspended above the top of the galvanized drum. This location is easier to maintain and eliminates the need for a wooden lid.

Bottom View

Pressure Valve
If possible, also install a pressure gauge in the house, such as on the cistern water line feeding the toilet. This makes checking the pump pressure much easier.

Pressure Valve Pipe Extension
The only purpose of this pipe is to get the pressure valve high enough so that it can be read without removing the pressure tank assembly from its storage drum.

Bar-B-Que Grill Base
It sounds odd, yet this is an easy-to-obtain item that is both durable and functional. Nuts, bolts, and large washers are used to affix the various components to the grill base. This system allows for great flexibility in positioning components without having to drill holes. When designing and building, use your imagination as to what might more easily solve a particular problem.

Risers were constructed by stacking two Simpson® plastic standoff bases end-to-end.

Electrical line to pump

Water lines to and from the pump are flexible in order to permit lifting the pump assembly out of the 50-gallon drum.

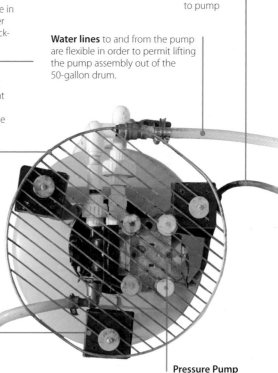

Pressure Pump

5. ADOBE

Earthen structures are found around the world. The interior thermal mass walls of this home are made of adobe bricks, which are nothing more than mud that has been poured into a form and then dried in the sun. Rammed earth is slightly damp earth mixed with a small amount of cement. It is tamped into wooden or metal wall forms that vary from 18" to 24" in thickness. Once compacted, the forms are removed, and the wall is self standing. Pressed adobe block is made by compressing the raw earth in a mold under extreme pressure. If these materials are not appropriate or not available in your area, thermal mass walls can be constructed of stone, brick, or any other dense and heavy material (see page 20).

Adobe bricks are available in three different forms: fully stabilized, semi-stabilized, and unstabilized. Fully stabilized adobe has enough asphalt emulsion added to the mix so that the block can sit in water for seven days and not absorb more than 2% of its weight in water. These adobe bricks cost more, so they are most commonly used only where they are required by code or where they will be taking the brunt of weather, such as the top layer of an outdoor adobe wall. A semi-stabilized adobe has less asphalt emulsion (about 3-5% by weight) and provides better weather resistance than pure mud. Unstabilized adobes have no asphalt emulsion and consist of pure mud. Semi-stabilized adobes are available from commercial adobe yards and are the most common.

The average adobe brick measures 4"x10"x14". Depending on how the adobe is oriented, the wall can be 10" thick (the most common) or 14" thick. This home has 10" and 24"-thick interior walls. The 24"-thick wall is made by alternating the bricks side by side using both the 10" and 14" widths (see pictures on page 69).

Mud mortar is used to hold the adobe bricks together. The mortar usually contains the same amount of stabilizer (asphalt emulsion) that is used in the brick itself. This is added to the water while mixing the mortar. The problem with asphalt emulsion is that it is a waste product from oil production and therefore is not an environmentally sound material. It adds a dubious ingredient to both the adobe brick itself and to the mortar. Other than that, adobe and other earthen materials are about as ecologically sound as you can get. The mix that was used for the earth plaster (see page 121) also works as an adobe mortar. Since all the adobe walls in this house are indoors, technically the stabilizing of the mortar was not an issue, as the walls are protected from the elements. If using adobe, consult with the local adobe experts and code as how best to stabilize the mortar for your particular project.

Mark the fully stabilized adobes so you can tell them apart from the semi-stabilized or unstabilized adobes. Otherwise, after some passage of time, it is likely that you will not remember which is which. The fully stabilized adobes are usually a little bit darker in color. Marking them removes the guesswork.

The traditional way to cut an adobe is to score the surface with the edge of your masonry trowel and then to break it on a rigid edge of a hard surface. You can also use a small pick or hatchet, as this will save the edge of your trowel.

DVD Location: 54 minutes 54 seconds

Another way is to score the adobe to a depth of about 1/2" by using a hand-held power saw with a masonry blade. This may give you a cleaner cut when you are learning to work with adobe and need more precision in making adobe bond-beam forms as shown on page 74. Yes, this is overkill. However, it does work. Always wear proper eye and ear protection when cutting adobes.

DVD Location: 59 minutes 26 seconds

See pages 122-123 for the mud-mixing procedure. Unlike with earth plaster, small stones up to 1/4" do not need to be sifted out of the mortar mix. We used wheat paste, instead of asphalt emulsion, as a method of making the mortar weather resistant. Asphalt emulsion is more common and can be added to the mix in the proportion of 3-5% by weight for semi-stabilized mortar. This amount will vary depending on the type of soil that is used. Too much emulsion will weaken the mud and make it crumble. The mortar can be mixed manually in a wheelbarrow or in a portable cement mixer. As always, follow your local codes as to the requirements for building with adobe in your area.

Speed leads (or story poles) are used as guides to ensure the walls will be true and straight. Although not necessary, they will significantly speed up the construction process. This system can be used for all types of masonry including stone, brick, cement block, and adobe. The speed lead consists of either a single, well-braced vertical pole for a 10"-thick adobe wall or two parallel poles for thicker walls.. Shown here is the speed lead for a 24"-thick wall. On the thicker walls, a string guide will be used on each side of the wall.

The poles are placed at both ends of the wall. Incremental marks are placed on each pole, indicating the thickness of the brick and mortar, with one mark for each layer. A water level (see page 37) is an excellent tool for marking a reference height on each pole and ensures that the marks are at the same height on all poles.

A nylon line is tightly stretched from one pole to the other. It must be tight enough to eliminate any sags in the middle. Otherwise your wall will dip in the middle as well. This mason's line then acts as a guide for positioning each layer of adobe or brick. When one layer is complete, the line is moved up to the next mark. If your poles are properly positioned and are true, your wall will be the same. The clip holding the line is homemade from wood. A metal fitting in an "L" shape would be more durable. The string is flush against the 2x4 post. The numbers indicate the course of adobes. The space between the lines is 4¾"—the thickness of the adobe, which is about 4", plus the height of the mortar.

The Parts Of An Adobe Wall

Wooden sill plate is bolted to the bond beam.

Bond beam

Adobe blocks

Mud mortar

Steel ladder can be placed every 6 courses unless otherwise determined by code.

The first course is fully stabilized adobe.

Rubble trench foundation

1 This first course uses fully stabilized adobe because of possible flooding and moisture absorption. It is set in cement mortar or in mud mortar that has been fully stabilized with asphalt emulsion. Either way, the mortar goes under and between the bricks.

2 Subsequent layers use mud mortar. Some builders use cement mortar for the entire wall. Mud will make a superior mud-to-mud bond between adobes and create a stronger homogeneous structure. The mortar is stiff enough that it will not be squeezed out by the weight of the adobe. You should be able to do 3-4 courses per day and still have the mortar support the weight of the wall without oozing out. The mud

can be shoveled or troweled into place and then smoothed to the approximate thickness by trowel or hand. Make the mortar a bit thicker in elevation than you need because the adobe will squeeze it down a bit. Mud tends to dry out your skin and be abrasive, so gloves are recommended.

Wide thermal mass walls, such as the 24" example to the right, are made by alternating the direction of the adobes. The direction of the adobes reverses at every layer in order to stagger the seams. Code here specified a minimum overlap of 4" from brick to brick.

It may be required to cut or trim adobes to fit into narrow or odd-shaped areas, such as around electrical outlet boxes.

3 Adobes are then lowered into position and wiggled into place, using the mason's line as a guide. This tends to make the mortar ooze out the sides. The joints are cleaned up with a trowel or glove, and that excess mortar is placed on top of the bricks for the next course.

The adobes are placed just short of touching the mason's line. If the bricks do touch the line, you may lose your straight reference guide. Periodically check the accuracy of your story poles to assure they have not been knocked out of vertical alignment.

4 Steel ladder, which is available from masonry suppliers, can be placed on every 4-6 courses for additional strength. Mud mortar and additional bricks are placed on top of the steel ladder.

5 The steel electrical boxes are screwed to a piece of scrap wood (around 1/2" thick). The wood extends out to either side and forms a solid mounting for the electrical box. Multiple outlets can be affixed to a single board. Work with your electrician and follow the current electrical code when wiring and placing boxes within the wall.

Electrical wiring is run within the adobe wall. Since adobe is dirt, code permits the use of UF (which stands for Underground Feeder) cable to run within the wall itself. The electrical cable is set at least 1.5" in from the outside, as mandated by code. This prevents nails from puncturing the wire at a later time. Allow a sufficient length of wire to extend from the box so that the electrician can readily wire up the outlets later on.

Adobes and mortar are then laid on top of the wire. If you need to get a wire from one level to the next, just stair step it to the desired level between the adobe joints.

6 It will sometimes be necessary to attach other elements to an adobe wall, which may include attaching a frame wall, shelving, and wooden bases for nichos. Presented here are a few different methods.

Gringo Blocks

A gringo block can be inserted into the wall in order to form a wooden nailing surface. For example, this could be used for attaching a frame wall. The gringo block is made out of 2x4s and is the same size as an adobe block. It is nailed together and, after it is positioned, it is filled with mud to form a solid unit.

The surface of the gringo block that is going to be used as a nailing surface must be sandwiched within the surrounding wood walls. This prevents the load of the wall from pulling out the piece that will be nailed into. In the gringo block to the right, the long side is the nailing surface, and it is captured within the shorter side pieces.

Anchor Bolts

Anchor bolts contain an "S" shape so that they cannot be pulled out. The straight section is threaded. The bolts are imbedded within cement mortar with the threaded side protruding a sufficient distance from the outside surface of the wall. These bolts will be locked into position between the layers of adobe.

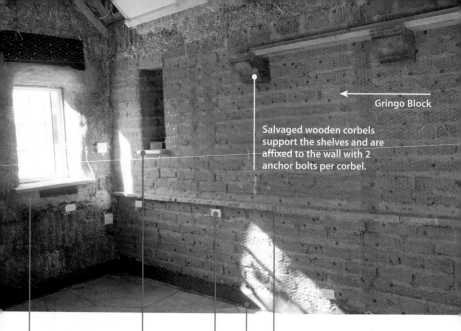

Gringo Block ←

Salvaged wooden corbels
support the shelves and are
affixed to the wall with 2
anchor bolts per corbel.

Flagstone wainscotting (see page 15)

Mortar base for baseboard tile (see page 131)

Electrical outlet. The box appears high on the wall because
a raised floor will be installed below.

The wooden shelf in this nicho was installed during the construction of the wall. Nails were hammered partway into the wood to act as "hooks"
when embedded in the wet mud mortar base.
The shelf was given a few coats of a weather-
resistant coating and then wrapped in plastic to
protect it from damage during construction. If the
side contacting the mud is not also coated, use
a sheet of tar paper to prevent the wood from
absorbing moisture from the mortar.

A cob nicho is under the flagstone window shelf. See
page 119 for how it was constructed and page 15 for
the completed nicho.

Flagstone wainscotting is added to one of the adobe walls as a visual element. This acts as a division between two different colors of earth plasters that will be applied in a later step. White earth plaster will be used above the flagstone, and brown below.

1. This shows the cut flagstone in position. It extends approximately 2" from the front surface of the wall. The finished depth will be less than this due to earth plaster that will be added in a later step. The flagstone pieces extend into the wall about 5".

2. The flagstone is scored to a depth of about 3/8" with a power saw fitted with a masonry blade. A piece of wood is used as a straight edge. The score is shallow in order to preserve a more natural edge for most of the thickness.

3. Using a brick set, which is like a giant chisel, the excess stone is broken away, leaving a natural-looking edge.

4 and 5. The flagstone is set into mud mortar. Adobe and mud mortar are then positioned behind and on top of the flagstone. Since the adobe is 4" thick, about 2" of mud mortar is added on top of the flagstone to match the height of the adobe behind it. This is seen as the darker mud in the photo to the right. Every course after this is laid by staggering the adobe seams.

7 The final step in completing the adobe wall is to install the bond beam. The most commonly used materials for constructing bond beams are wood and concrete. We chose concrete in order to conserve wood and gain thermal mass. Three different methods were used to create the forms. Each has its pros and cons.

Adobe Bond Beam Form For A Wide Adobe Wall

For the 2'-thick adobe wall, the forms for the bond beam were also made from adobes. They were cut in half on the long dimension and stood on end to form the 6" high concrete bond beam cavity that is code in New Mexico. Due to the 24" width of the wall, code says that the bond beam only had to cover two-thirds of the width, which permitted the use of adobe as a form. Note the use of a speed lead (left photo) to ensure a level beam. This is important since roof trusses will be affixed to the bond beam.

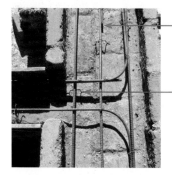

3 parallel pieces of #4 rebar were used in this 24" wide wall

Steel chairs are used to raise the rebar about 2" above the base.

Concrete is mixed and then lifted to the top of the wall with buckets. The concrete is screeded across the top to form a surface level with the adobe forms. It is then worked with a wooden trowel for further smoothing. Anchor bolts are set within the wet concrete. These will be used to secure a 2x6 sill plate whose function is to act as an anchor plate for the roof trusses. (See page 81.)

Wood Frame Form

For the 10"-wide adobe wall, a wood bond beam form was used. Scrap 1" thick lumber was used to create the 6" depth. Several steps were used here to hold the forms together. Holes were drilled 6" down from the top of the wood sides. Then wire was crisscrossed back and forth. This made a base that prevented the forms from sliding down. Cross braces are used on top. An adjustable clamp is used on the end to squeeze the wood against the sides of the adobe. A gringo block was used for attaching an additional brace. A level was used to assure that the form was level across the long run and from side to side. The forms were removed when the concrete had cured.

DVD Location: 1 hour 00 minutes 28 seconds

Bond-Beam-Block Form

For the 10"-wide adobe wall in the workshop, bond beam block was used. This is a commercially available product that resembles a standard cement block. It eliminates the need for wood. The block itself becomes the form. The three short cross members of the block have knockouts which, when removed, become the supports for the rebar. This eliminated the need for the chairs that were used in previous examples. The blocks are mortared together atop the adobe wall. At corners, a section was cut from one side so that the rebar can make the bend. The forms were then filled with concrete.

The down side is that bond beam block is a bit more tedious to install, and the bond beam ended up being thicker than 6", which is more than is needed.

DVD Location: 1 hours 03 minutes 04 seconds

In this house, the load of the roof is supported by a post-and-beam structure. The straw bales are used for infill only and do not take any structural load. Some local building codes allow the load of the roof to sit directly on the straw bale walls. When this is the case, the straw bale walls are assembled first, and the roof is added later. There are pros and cons to both methods.

In the post-and-beam method demonstrated here, a series of 4x4 posts can be spaced up to 8' apart if using a 4x8 beam. The posts usually end up being closer than this because they are also used to frame windows and doors.

There are only two conventional stud-frame walls in this home. Their purpose is to permit the installation of plumbing. Running water pipes through adobe and straw bale should be avoided, as water can be damaging to both. A frame wall is also easier to deal with if a plumbing problem should later develop.

If possible, purchase wood that is sustainably grown from a certified supplier. Even in a straw bale home, such as this, there is still a considerable amount of wood used above the walls. Sustainably grown wood does not use old-growth trees, and the timber is harvested in an ecologically sound manner.

Temporary bracing to keep the posts plumb

4x8 perimeter beam   4x4 vertical post   Pre-engineered roof truss
Metal tie

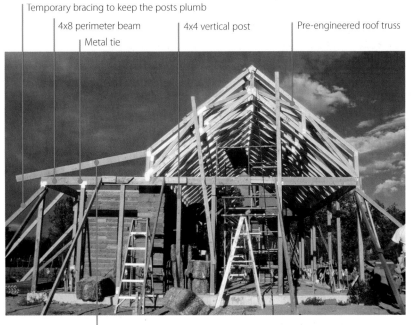

2x6 rafter on north side

1   The vertical 4x4 posts of the post-and-beam framing are installed as shown. Brackets are attached with nuts to the bolts in the foundation after a string is stretched from corner to corner to ensure that all brackets are in line with each other.

The metal riser will keep the post from contacting the concrete and absorbing moisture. The posts are then nailed and/or bolted to the bracket. A level is used to make sure the posts are plumb in both directions.

Metal riser ——

Temporary cross bracing is added to two sides. This is very important in order to keep the post plumb during the construction process. After the roof trusses are installed, these temporary braces are removed.

When all of the 4x4s are in position, one post is marked with the desired cut-off height. A water level (see page 37) is then used to mark the same height on all remaining posts. This ensures that all posts are cut to this reference height, regardless of slight variations in the foundation height.

2 The perimeter beam is made from two 2x8s nailed together with staggered joints. The resulting 4x8 was chosen over a 4x10 because it avoided the use of larger-dimensional lumber. 4x10s and larger usually come from older-growth, 18"+ diameter trees. The 4x8 required the posts to be 8' apart, as opposed to 10' spacing of the 4x10s. This continuous beam runs the full length of the house and is very strong. At each joint, a plywood stiffener was added for additional strength.

Plywood stiffener at joint

Temporary 2x4 retainers are attached to the outside of the posts so that the beam does not fall off when it is placed in position. If these braces do not extend beyond the straw bale wall, they can be left in place. The long beam is then carefully lifted into position by as many people as are necessary. It is initially nailed to the corner posts only. The center posts are made plumb with a level, and the beam is then nailed to them as well. Metal connector plates are now added to secure the connection.

Additional Ways To Frame For Straw Bale

Alternative materials for beams include box beams (which are on-site-constructed hollow beams), steel studs, and engineered structural lumber. The latter is a manufactured replacement for solid wood beams and is made from smaller trees and waste wood. Engineered structural lumber includes *laminated veneer lumber* (dimensional lumber made of thin layers of wood glued together, much like plywood) and *manufactured wood I-beams* (which are typically made of a center web of plywood capped with laminated veneer lumber). Always consult with an architect or structural engineer as to the proper material for your project.

Steel framing is used for the first straw bale post office in the U.S., located in Corrales, New Mexico. The interior walls are finished in wallboard attached directly to the steel studs.
(Designed by Studio Southwest Architects, formerly known as DCSW)

This is the completed post-and-beam framing as seen from the north side.

Tip

large nail is used as a pivot

brace for fulcrum

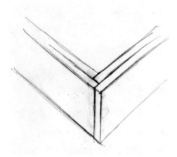

Above: By sighting down the beam with a string guide, it is easy to see that the beam is not perfectly straight. Bends can be straightened with a large lever to pull the beam into place. It consists of attaching a temporary 2x4 lever to the temporary diagonal brace. The beam is then pulled into alignment. When straight, the diagonal brace is secured firmly to the ground with additional stakes, and the lever is removed.

Left: Detail of how two perimeter beams intersect at corners

3 A 2x6 wood sill plate is attached to the top of the concrete bond beam on the adobe walls. Holes are drilled in the wood to line up with the bolts imbedded in the concrete. Nuts and washers secure the wood to the beam. The purpose of the sill plate is to provide a nailing surface for attaching the roof trusses. The anchor bolts must be located so that they do not end up at a truss location.

4 The 2x6 wood-frame walls contain both the fresh-water plumbing, the drain, waste, and vent (DWV) plumbing, and the electrical wiring. There are many books which contain helpful construction techniques for framing stud walls such as these.

	Drain vent pipe to the roof
	Natural-gas pipe for the mechanical room
	Electrical outlet and wiring
	Fresh-water stub
	Copper pipe stub for cistern water supply to the toilet.
	Toilet drain

Above: This wall divides the bathroom from the mechanical room (as seen from the bathroom side). The wall will be thoroughly insulated with blown-in insulation. The on-demand gas water heater is directly on the other side of this wall, which greatly cuts down on water-and-energy waste. Plumbing-run distances are very short to each fixture. This reduces the cost of the plumbing because less time and material are needed to install the system. **Right:** The hot-water lines in the ceiling are insulated with foam and are located within the insulated cavity below the roof. The black pipe is a natural-gas line and therefore is not insulated.

5 With the walls in place, the ceiling joists are installed. The 2x6 joists in the entry room and kitchen will be left exposed. Within the areas where the connection of joists to the beam will be hidden, metal brackets are used for maximum strength. The north storage/utility room and bathroom will have wallboard affixed to the joists to hide them.

The 2x6 ceiling joists in the kitchen and entry room also support the loft floor.

Left: The loft floor is made of aspen wood. Aspen is fast growing and is a more ecologically sound alternative to pine, oak, and many other woods. The downside is that it is very soft. Since this is not a high traffic area, that will not be a problem. The disadvantage of installing the finished floor at this early stage is that it has to be protected from rain and physical damage throughout the construction process.

Loft area on floor plan

6 The steep pitched roof over the main living area is constructed of pre-engineered trusses. A pre-engineered truss is ecologically sound in that small dimensional lumber is used instead of 2x10's and larger. For this roof, only 2x4's were used. The specifications of the roof should be given to a truss manufacturer who will engineer, assemble, and deliver the completed trusses to the site on a specified date. This approach saves a considerable

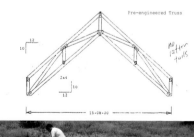

amount of time. The truss depth was designed to accommodate a minimum of R-55 insulation. Small trusses, such as used here, can be carried by two people.

The position of each truss is marked on the top of the 4x8 perimeter beam and on the sill plates on top of the adobe walls. One by one, the trusses are lifted into place, nailed, and secured with metal brackets. Temporary cross braces are used to keep everything rigid until the roof sheeting is installed. This entire installation was completed within a day.

This temporary bracing will be removed when the roof is sheeted.

2x6 rafter tails are attached to the trusses with about an 18" overlap.

1. Hurricane straps are used to connect the trusses to the walls. **2.** This is the truss connection to the wood plate on top of the adobe wall. **3.** The pre-assembled trusses do not include the roof overhang for the control of solar gain. To construct the overhang, a 2x6 rafter tail is attached directly to the truss. This saves a considerable amount of wood since the upper member of the truss is constructed out of a 2x4 instead of a 2x6. The 2x6 rafter tail is cut to the proper length when all of the pieces are in place. A 2x6 looks better than a 2x4 on the finished home.

DVD Location: 1 hours 14 minutes 45 seconds

7 The roof over the north side of the house is a gentle slope that is in contrast to the steeper pitch of the main roof. The joists on this side are assembled by hand and are attached to the pre-engineered truss on one side and to the 4x8 beam on the other.

Floor plan showing north rooms and roof slope

1. The sloped roof on the north side of the building is made of 2x6s that are notched to rest squarely on the perimeter beam. **2**. Since these joists are exposed under the roof overhang, it is important to make joists perpendicular to the beam for appearance. A giant fork was made to easily twist any warps out of the joist. **3.** Metal hurricane straps were used to mechanically form a rigid connection between the roof and the walls. This is particularly important when large roof overhangs exist, as wind reaching under the eaves can exert a lot of upward force.

The overhangs on the gable ends were pre-assembled on the ground. These units were lifted into position and bolted to the roof trusses. This is just one of several methods that can be used for constructing roof overhangs.

Metal roof sheeting

Tar paper (roofing felt)

1x4 lumber for the overhangs

Oriented strand board (OSB), exterior-grade plywood, or a compressed straw-based sheeting.

8 Three different elements make up the final roof assembly. First, a layer of OSB, which stands for "oriented strand board," is screwed to the trusses. This is followed by a layer of roofing felt, also known as tar paper. The final layer is corrugated, galvanized metal sheeting. Note that the oriented strand board stops at the roof overhang. 1x4 lumber is used instead. This was done purely for visual appeal. When seen from below, the wooden slats with the exposed metal roofing create a more pleasing appearance than the OSB sheeting (see page 89).

A metal roof was chosen for a variety of reasons. Metal roofs are very durable and long-lasting, and they have an aesthetic history in this region. They also provide a clean, rainwater-collection surface for cisterns. Asphalt-based materials should be avoided since they will contaminate the rainwater. Metal sheeting is trimmed with a rotary saw equipped with a metal-cutting blade. Small cuts are easily made with tin snips.

Greener Sheeting

Interior-grade OSB and plywood contain adhesives that incorporate urea-formaldeyide. Formaldehyde is toxic and can outgas into the occupied area of the home. It is also an environmental problem at the manufacturing plant. Exterior-grade OSB sheeting and plywood use a more environmentally sound phenol-formaldehyde adhesive. Therefore, *exterior-grade* plywood and OSB sheeting should be specified for your construction project. If this is not possible, the sheeting can be painted with a sealer to help cut down on outgassing. Greener substitutes for plywood and OSB sheeting, such as structural panels made of compressed straw, are now appearing on the market and should also be considered.

The OSB comes in 4x8 sheets. The temporary cross braces are removed before the sheeting is positioned. Always wear a safety harness when working on the roof and other high places.

A metal "H" clip is easily slipped into place between the joints of the sheeting. They are positioned in the space between the trusses. This prevents the sheets from warping and adds rigidity. The small gap created by the clip also acts as an expansion joint between the panels.

The width of one nail between each vertical joint allows the sheeting to expand and contract with changes in temperature and humidity. This nail is tapped just enough to hold it in place. Once the sheeting is permanently secured, it is removed.

Each sheet is tack nailed to hold it in position. It is then permanently fastened with screws along the truss lines. A chalk line can be snapped to show the position of the truss underneath. Screws may take a bit more time but will provide more secure connections than conventional nails.

Once the sheeting is installed, 2x4 bracing is added to the area within the trusses. These braces run the entire length of the roof and will provide a much more rigid structure.

NOTE: Since the straw bale wall system we used required hammering vertical rebar into the tops of the straw bales (as is required by New Mexico code and some others), the metal roofing had to be installed after the bales were in place. This made it necessary to remove some of the lower panels of OSB sheeting in order to gain access to the top of the bales. If you are allowed to eliminate the use of internal vertical pins within your straw bales (see page 96), you can complete the roof before any bales are stacked. This is very desirable since the bales are then protected from rain as soon as installed.

9 Tar paper (roofing felt) is stapled to the sheeting. Start at the bottom of the roof and work upwards. Each layer overlaps the one below it. This keeps leaks through the metal sheeting from penetrating below the tar paper. Any water then flows to the lower edge of the roof.

10

Metal roofing is installed per the manufacturer's instructions. The screws used here incorporate a rubber gasket that aids in making the screw holes water tight. The tip of the screw is very sharp so that it will penetrate the sheet metal with the downward pressure of the drill. Any water that does penetrate a screw hole will run down over the roofing felt underlayment to the bottom edge of the roof.

rubber gasket

Details

Wherever possible, keep roof penetrations to a minimum. All are all potential locations for leaks. The vent for the gas hot-water heaters can be seen in the left and center photos. A flexible rubber boot conforms to the corrugated roofing and seals the opening. To the right is a plumbing vent which is thoroughly sealed with silicone caulk beneath the boot. All of the drain plumbing in the house vents to this single pipe, thus eliminating multiple roof holes.

The ridge vent is a visual element and also aids in releasing warm air from the roof cavity above the insulation. It uses a simple 2x4 framing system. The sides were covered with window screen bug guards before the sheet metal vent panels were installed. As an experiment, operable vents at the top of the vaulted ceiling can release hot indoor air into the ridge vent. It turned out the windows provide adequate ventilation, and the interior vents are not needed.

Above: The roof of the porch and all of the overhangs take advantage of the contrast between wood and corrugated sheet metal.

Below Left: The bases of the porch support pillars are made of stone. Their wood posts are constructed from salvaged 6x6s. **Below Right:** Attaching the wood posts to the stone bases was accomplished by cutting in half U-shaped metal brackets. **Bottom Left:** Both halves were then imbedded in concrete within the stone base. A bit of soap was rubbed onto the metal to make it easier to slip on the 6x6. **Bottom Middle:** The post was slotted with an electric reciprocating saw. The hole locations for the metal brackets were marked and drilled into the wood. **Bottom Right:** Large bolts were used to tie everything together. The wood does not contact the stone because the metal brackets hold it 3/8" above in order to prevent the absorption of moisture. This approach emphasizes the mechanical connection as a design feature instead of trying to hide it.

The technology of building straw bale walls for homes is constantly changing. Experiments with new methods are being conducted around the world. Some locations have specific building codes related to straw bale construction. Some do not. Many areas require that the straw bale walls may not take the load of the roof, and therefore the bales act as infill to a post-and-beam-type structure. Other areas allow the load of the roof to be carried by the straw bales themselves. Certain climates may require different construction techniques. Before drawing up plans for your home, research what is the best method for your location. This will be based on what has already been done in your area and what the current research shows to be the best methods. The bottom line is to make sure that your home meets or exceeds the structural requirements of the local building codes and protects the bales from excessive moisture, which is the primary enemy of straw bale.

If possible, you may want to attend a straw bale workshop to gain first-hand knowledge of working with straw. Local experts can also be hired to hold a workshop for your home or to act as a consultant or contractor on your project. The method presented here is just one of many ways of building with straw bale. The system we used followed both the local straw bale building codes and the procedures being used in the state at the time of construction. You may find, as we did, that certain building codes are not necessarily geared toward what is considered the ideal practice in the straw bale or green-building world. Guidelines for green building are slowly being developed. Part of the construction process is learning how to work with the system. Some alternatives to the techniques we used are pointed out in this chapter.

The bales are stacked on wooden pallets to protect them from ground moisture. Heavy-duty tarps, secured by ropes, are used for protection from rain. It is important to occasionally check the cover material for holes, as UV rays from the sun will eventually damage the tarps. Two layers of tarps are used here. Storing bales under a roof is even better.

Top waterproof membrane

4x4 post

Window frame

Top waterproof membrane

Straw bales with alternating vertical joints laid like brick

Metal cross brace for frame

Wire stucco netting for lower band of stucco

Straw bales come from food crops such as wheat, barley, and oats. During harvesting, the upper nutritional part is removed and used for food. The lower part is usually discarded and becomes another waste problem. Many farmers are now selling this material for use in straw bale homes. When used for structures, the bales are tightly compressed and are held together with polypropylene string. Depending on the size of the bale, they will be either 2-string or 3-string. The 2-string bales, which were used for this project, weighed around 35 pounds each.

Straw bales are not always available year-round. Check for availability well in advance. It is also important to specify the size of the bales. Our supplier offered 2-string and 3-string bales. The 2-string bales were 18" wide and came in both a 14" and 16" height. The 16" bale height means that fewer bales would need to be stacked.

This is a typical 2-string straw bale.

16" tall

18" wide

36" long

1 A moisture barrier is placed on the footing to prevent moisture from wicking up from the concrete. Use 15-pound asphalt roofing felt (unless otherwise specified by code). Remember that the foundation was poured 2" higher than the floor in order to protect the bales from pooling water from unexpected sources. Any penetrations through the moisture barrier, as well as all joints in the barrier, are sealed with asphalt or silicone caulk.

2 The straw bales are pushed down on the rebar embedded in the foundation (see pages 30 and 38). There are two rebars per bale, and they extend vertically through 1½ bales. The bale is then kicked and nudged into position. For this home the bales were placed so that the wall thickness was 18".

A string is used as a guide to keep the straw bales running in a straight line. The string indicates the outside of the foundation (including the foam insulation), which is also the outside surface of the bales. The string can be affixed to the vertical posts of the framing. The bales are placed just short of touching the string.

Fire Safety

Tightly bound straw bale walls are quite resistant to fire. Tests show that they have a better fire rating than most wood-frame walls. Loose straw, such as that which collects on the ground while working with bales, is very flammable. It is important to rake up any loose straw and place it in a sealed container. This loose straw can be saved for the upcoming earth plaster mix, but it must be appropriately stored away from the structure.

3 Notching is required where a bale meets a post. It is possible to design a home where the posts are either inside or outside of the bales. This will change the engineering of the building as well as how the exposed posts work visually with the overall design.

Notching is not particularly hard to do, but it does add some time. To begin, place the straw bale in its proper location and mark the location of the post with paint.

It is likely that some of the strings which hold the bale together will fall within the area to be notched. The strings can be tied back by using polypropylene twine to pull the two lines together. Remember to tie them together on both sides of the bale.

An electric chain saw is then used to cut the notch to the desired depth. A handsaw can also be used, although it is considerably slower and more labor intensive. When cutting with a chain saw, the two vertical cuts are made first. The saw can then be plunged in horizontally to complete the notch.

The straw bale is then wedged into position around the post. The notched bales should fit snugly around the posts and should also be very snug against the sides of adjoining bales.

Mark

Tie

Notch

Place

4 Shown here is one method of attaching the bales to the posts. Expanded-metal lath is nailed to the posts. Landscape staples are used to pin the lath to the straw bales. These staples are available from plant nurseries and landscape-supply stores and come in 6" and 9" lengths. You will be using hundreds of these, so it pays to buy them in bulk.

Another method involves tying the bales to the posts with polypropylene twine. Some codes require that U-shaped pins made of rebar be used at each corner bale.

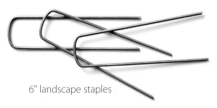

6" landscape staples

5 The average bale is about 36" in length. Often there are places where a straw bale must be split in half in order to fit the space. An example is shown to the right where multiple half-bales are used between the window and the door. Splitting a bale requires that the bale be retied with polypropylene line before the original strings are cut. Otherwise, the bale will spring apart and lose its tight compaction. The new strings are threaded through the center of the bale with a large needle and tightly tied. Please see the DVD video for a demonstration on how to split a bale. From the main menu, go to "Construction Details" and then choose "How To Split a Straw Bale."

Half bales used between 2 posts

6 When the wall is four courses high, stakes are hammered down through the bales. These stakes consist of ½" #4 rebar. There are two rebars per bale. By the sixth course, there will be 2 groups of 4 rebars going through each bale. The purpose of this pinning system is to tie all of the bales together into one unit.

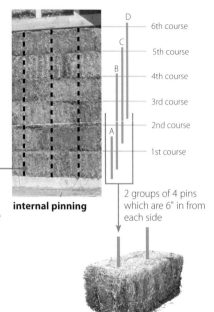

internal pinning

Represents a group of 4 internal pins. The first 5' pin is hammered in at the 4th course, and 1 additional pin will be inserted at each course thereafter. Pin A was embedded in the foundation (see page 38).

D — 6th course
C — 5th course
B — 4th course
— 3rd course
— 2nd course
A — 1st course

2 groups of 4 pins which are 6" in from each side

Above: One alternative **external pinning** method uses wooden stakes or bamboo (represented in red) tied to the bales. These can be installed after the bales are stacked. Other methods include wrapping the bale walls in a sturdy welded wire mesh. This adds stability in seismic areas, although it does introduce metal and may not be desirable if using earth plasters (see page 116). Straw bale construction is still evolving. Techniques may vary from region to region.

Another approach

Pinning is often required by code. New Mexico code specified the use of internal rebar pins. The problem is that rebar adds a high-embodied energy material to the wall, and there is concern that the metal may sweat in cold and damp climates and introduce moisture into the bales. Many builders are using alternatives to this method where code permits. If allowed, you may prefer a natural material such as wooden stakes or bamboo. Some also consider this a better holistic approach in that it eliminates metal. (See page 116 for more on metal in buildings.)

The best reason for using an alternative to internal pinning is that it will allow you to completely finish the roof before installing the bales. This is a huge advantage in that the bales will have better protection from rain. We were not able to install the final metal roofing until all of the bales were installed because the OSB sheeting on the roof would interfere with hammering in the rebars on the upper bales.

Take a 36" long by ¼" round steel stock and mark the location of the bend about 6" from one end. With an inexpensive gas torch, such as that used for soldering copper plumbing, heat the location of the bend until it glows. Quickly insert the rod in a rigid vice and hammer in a 90° bend. Remove the rod from the vice and immerse the bend in cold water. Use a grinder to flatten both sides of the tip to a thickness of about 1/8". Next grind a point at the tip. Drill two holes in the flat section. The holes must be wide enough to accommodate the polypropylene twine for restringing the bales. To save time, ready-made straw bale needles, such as those made by Straw Bale Innovations, are also available.

7 There are multiple ways to frame a window. Two methods are shown here. This home used the vertical posts for the side supports of the larger windows. The posts are spaced specifically to accommodate the width of the windows. This type of window framing is very similar to that of a conventionally framed home.

4x8 top perimeter beam

Header consisting of two 2x4s

4x4 post. The posts are positioned to double as the side framing for the window.

Rough sill

This void was created by the window framing not being at a full-bale height. The area can be filled with partial bales of straw or a clay-straw mix. In our case, cob was used inside to create a nicho below the window. (See page 119 for how this was done.) Although the window size or height could have been adjusted to avoid this, it would have conflicted with other design elements on the interior of the home. Sometimes it is worth doing a bit more work in order to achieve the design you desire.

Smaller windows can be supported by the straw itself. This window buck is a "floater" in that it is suspended within the bales. This particular window takes advantage of a post on one side and uses long pins to secure the frame to the bales on the other. 2x6 lumber is used to form the buck. The interior dimensions of the window buck are slightly greater than the window unit itself. The dimensions are specified by the window manufacturer.

Two holes are drilled into the side of the window buck where it meets the straw bale. The buck is then secured to the bales by hammering in rebar or wood pegs. The rebar was scrap from the foundation and bond beams. Wood dowels or bamboo could also be used. If a post had not been supporting the other side of the buck, pins would be used there as well.

This long horizontal window in the bathroom was also able to take advantage of a post on one side. The right side has a support dropping down from the upper beam for additional rigidity. For additional strength to support this longer window, the upper header of this window buck consists of two parallel 2x6s.

8 A shelf for holding straw bales is installed above all windows, doors, and wall openings. The shelves are made of OSB or plywood sheeting (use exterior-grade structural sheeting to prevent formaldehyde from outgassing to the indoor air space (see page 86). The sheeting is reinforced with 2x4 lumber.

Window buck: A simple wood frame that is sized to the frame dimensions as specified for the manufactured window unit that will be installed.

Shelves for straw bales are placed over all wall openings. For additional support, 2x lumber drops down from the rafters. The shelves also rest on the bales below.

Split and retied bales were then used to fit between the rafters. Use only tightly compacted bales and partial bales in this area. Do not use loose straw in open areas around the rafters. Loose straw is flammable if exposed to an ignition source. Tightly compacted-and-tied bales are resistant to combustion.

For this upper wall area, the bales are turned on end to snugly fit between the two trusses on the gable ends.

DVD Location: 1 hour 28 minutes 54 seconds

9 By the end of the two-day workshop, over 80% of the straw bales were in place. Additional work included bullnosing around windows and doors with an electric chain saw. The chain saw is also used to level out the sides of the walls where needed. Leveling out the walls results in more efficient plastering, as there are fewer irregularities to fill with mud or plaster.

10 Under windows, the top straw bale is protected by a waterproof barrier to ensure that the bales will not get wet from a window leak. 15-pound roofing felt (tar paper) is used across the top and then folded down both sides by about 6".

The rebar will anchor the base for the flagstone window seat to the wall.

The top layer of straw bales has a moisture barrier to protect against roof leaks.

Moisture-resistant non-CFC insulation (leftover foam from the foundation) is used on the outside wall under the window buck. Ultimately, cement mortar or cob will be used in this area as a base for flagstone window seats. The insulation forms a thermal break to the outside for increased energy efficiency. The tar paper protects the bale from window leaks and from moisture from the cement mortar that will secure the window seat (see page 119). The rebar anchors the mortar base to the straw bale wall. It is standard procedure to wrap dimensional lumber with tar paper wherever it will be in contact with stucco or earth plaster.

Left: This window opening is the exterior view of the same window shown above.

The moisture barrier folds down 6" over the side of the straw bale to deflect rainwater leaks to the outside.

The stucco lath for the lower area of stucco that will be installed later

Diagonal Cross Bracing For The Post-and-Beam Framing

When the straw bale walls are complete, a strap is secured to the bolt on the exterior of the foundation. (See page 39 to see how the bolt was installed.)

A hole is drilled in the strap in order to insert a nut and bolt. The head of the bolt is then slipped on to the end of a crowbar.

The crowbar is used as a lever to pull the strap as tight as possible. If there is any slack in the strap, it will not serve its purpose.

Above: The metal strapping is in place, and the rain gutters are hooked up to the cistern. **Right:** The steel strap must be stretched very tightly. Where necessary, cut away the straw so that the strap is not pushed outward. **Far Right**: An extra 2x4 block fills out the gap between the straps and the recessed post. The diagonal strapping is nailed where it crosses any structural framing.

The electricity in this home is generated entirely by sunlight falling on photovoltaic panels on the south-facing roof. It is an elegant system: no fossil fuels are burned; no pollution is generated; it is quiet and free of maintenance (except for the lead-acid storage batteries); there are no moving parts. Although utility-generated electrical power is available on the street, I chose not to hook up to it at the time the home was constructed. Due to recent policy changes at the electric company, it would now make economic sense to tie the PV system into the grid. This would have eliminated the need for, and cost of, a large battery storage bank. The batteries are capable of supplying power to the home for up to 3 cloudy days (an unusual event in this part of the world).

The electrical system in a conventional home in the United States, Canada, and Mexico provides 120 volts AC. The voltage output of the banks of photo-voltaic panels is usually 12, 24, or 48 volts DC. This low-voltage DC electrical power is then converted, using a device called an inverter, to 120 volts AC. Once the electricity leaves the inverter, a PV-powered home is essentially wired the same as a conventional utility-powered home.

Electricians were hired who were proficient in working with photovoltaic systems and in wiring straw bale and adobe walls. We mounted the photovoltaic devices ourselves, and they did the wiring and final system hookups.*

Commercial photovoltaic (PV) panels are 10-12% efficient. That means about 90% of the sunlight hitting the panels is going unused. Year after year, the overall trend is that the cost of PV panels goes down while the efficiency goes up. The cost-versus-power output is now within reach of the homeowner. If your home is quite a distance from the nearest utility pole, a PV system might be the most ecological and economical way to go.

There are other options to PV power that may be even more economical. If your average wind speed is about 12 mph or more, wind power may be the best option. It is also possible to combine wind and PV power generation. If the up-front cost of generating your own electrical power is a problem, see if your local utility company offers the option of purchasing wind power or some other cleanly generated electricity directly from them. This usually adds a nominal additional charge to your monthly utility bill. Some utilities, such as those in California, offer significant rebates on the cost of installing clean energy-generation systems for residential use. This may lower the cost enough to make wind-or-solar generated electricity a viable option for your home.

* It is interesting to note that the local building codes did permit an owner/builder to do his or her own electrical work. The requirement was that the owner/builder had to take a written test on the national electrical codes. This pertains only to the homeowner, so friends and/or relatives cannot take the test and then do the electrical work for you. House building has enough challenges to deal with, and electrical wiring was one task I was more than happy to turn over to the professionals.

The photovoltaic system installed in this home

The PV panels are rated 900 watts at 24 volts DC. The battery bank consists of twelve 6 volt, L-16 wet-cell lead-acid batteries. They are wired in series and parallel to create 1,050 amp hours of storage capacity at 24 volts DC. A sine wave inverter converts the 24 volts DC to 120 volts AC. The inverter can supply up to 4,000 watts of continuous power (the length of time being limited by the size of the batteries). The total equipment cost (less labor) was about $10,000.

The power tools used in building this home were all run by sunlight-generated electricity. It is a great feeling to be able to power electric cement mixers, power saws, sanders, grinders, and drills—all from an on-site clean power source. The small workshop, which was built before the house, became the place to store tools and to act as temporary housing for the photovoltaic system. The PV panels were initially mounted on the workshop's roof, and the batteries were inside.

Below is a schematic of a typical off-grid photovoltaic electrical system. A grid-intertie system uses the electrical grid as the battery and adds power to, or takes it from, the grid as needed.

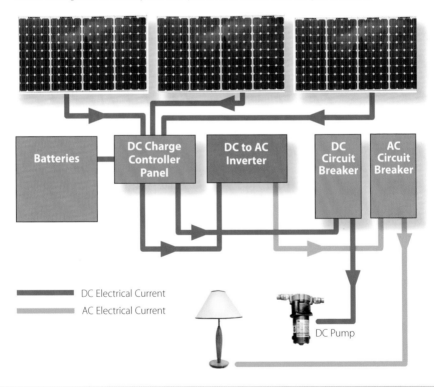

Amp hour: A measure of electrical energy in a battery equal to the battery current in amperes (amps) multiplied by the time in hours that the current flows. A current of 20 amps flowing for 1 hour would be 20 amp hours. 1 amp flowing for 20 hours would also be 20 amp hours.

Design considerations for a PV-powered home

The following suggestions will make any home more energy-efficient, even if you are buying your electrical power from a utility company. The suggestions are essential for a photovoltaic-powered system in order to reduce the size and cost of the PV equipment. Many PV systems are larger and more expensive than they need to be. This is sometimes caused by putting insufficient emphasis on purchasing energy-efficient appliances.

1. The design of an alternative energy system starts with choosing energy-efficient appliances. A few extra dollars spent on Energy Star-rated appliances could reduce the cost of the PV system by thousands of dollars. Pay particular attention to refrigerators and lighting, as these will typically use more power per year than anything else. Use only compact fluorescent lighting and/or LED lighting throughout the home. In a standard incandescent bulb, 90% of the energy leaves the bulb as heat, not light. It costs more to run an incandescent bulb than a comparable compact fluorescent or LED light. Despite their higher purchase costs, compact fluorescents are four times more efficient and last nine to thirteen times longer than incandescents. Therefore, fluorescents more than pay for themselves over their lifetimes.

2. Many appliances draw a few watts of power even when they are turned off. This continuous power drain is called a phantom load and is a waste of power, particularly when you generate your own electricity. Therefore, plug appliances, such as televisions, stereo systems, DVD players, computers, or any item with a phantom load, into an electrical outlet with a wall switch. In this home, the electrical outlet for the entertainment center can be turned off when the stereo or TV is not being used. A small lamp with a 4 watt bulb (see picture to above right) is connected to the same circuit. When the wall switch is on, the lamp adds a pleasant background glow. This light is a reminder to turn the switch off after watching the television or listening to the stereo. If the light is off, the electrical outlet is off, and therefore there are no phantom loads.

3. Properly sizing your power system will keep the cost down. The best way to do this is to measure the power you currently use for your existing appliances. A small and economical power-measuring device, such as the Kill-A-Watt™ meter (made by P3), will show you exactly how much power is used to do a load of wash, to run the refrigerator for a week, or to watch television for an hour. Just plug the appliance into the meter and note the current or long-term power drawn in watts, volts, and kilowatt-hours (the cumulative amount of watts used in an hour).

Energy Star: A set of guidelines set by the United States Environmental Protection Agency (EPA) to rate appliances that meet or exceed federal standards for energy efficiency. The program helps businesses and individuals lower their energy bills and protect the environment through the reduction of greenhouse gas emissions.

1 Electrical plans are drawn for the entire home. This drawing is a complete schematic of all of the circuits, switches, outlets, and built-in lighting fixtures. If your home will include any low-voltage DC circuits, the plans should show this as well. With the completed plan, the electrician will be able to give you an accurate quote for parts and labor.

Prices for electrical work vary widely. It is a good idea to obtain multiple bids. References are also very helpful in choosing an electrical contractor. Our primary electrician worked on an hourly basis plus cost of materials. He came highly recommended, and this payment method worked very well. A second contractor was hired for the final hookup of the photovoltaic system, as the first contractor had a previous commitment to install a PV system in Antarctica. The second contractor worked on a fixed-quote basis, which also worked very well.

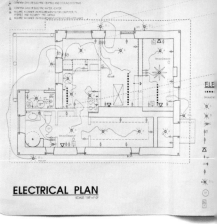

ELECTRICAL PLAN

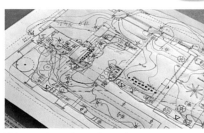

This top photo shows the preliminary electrical plan. It was greatly modified by the electrician (lower photo) to incorporate more circuits. Additional switches were also added to deal with phantom loads. DC circuits for the cistern pump and the circulation pump for the heating system were also drawn in.

2 Electrical code requires that the wiring be at least 1½" below the surface of the straw bale walls. UF (which stands for Underground Feeder) cable is used within both the straw bale and adobe walls. This moisture-resistant wire is designed to permit burying in the ground. The wire is either inserted in the joints between the bales, or an electric chain saw can be used to cut a slot. See page 70 for details on wiring adobe walls.

A chain saw is used to cut channels in the straw bale wall for the electrical wiring.

3 A wooden stake is affixed to the electrical boxes. Metal boxes are the ultimate in durability, although many prefer plastic boxes. These metal boxes are modular so multiple units can be screwed together if you need more switches. A hole for the box is carved out of the straw with a serrated knife. The box and stake are then hammered into the straw bale wall. The front face of the box is positioned a little forward of the straw bale surface. The distance is determined by the thickness of the plaster you will be using.

When installing heavier fixtures, such as outdoor lights that are subjected to high wind loads, a stouter attachment may be necessary. In this case the electrical box is affixed to a 2x piece of lumber which spans two posts.

2x6 wood support

4 To pass electrical wire through a straw bale wall, the wire is taped to a straw bale needle (see page 97) and pushed through to the other side.

5 For running wire through frame walls and ceilings, holes are drilled through the wood studs or ceiling joists, staying at least of 1½" away from any edge that might later be nailed or screwed into. The wires are then pulled through and directed toward the next receptacle or to the circuit-breaker panel.

The cable used here is called "Romex." It is not suitable for wet or damp locations. It is easier to bend than UF cable, so it is generally used wherever wire will go through frame walls.

6 The entire photovoltaic system was removed from the temporary location on the workshop to its final location on the roof of the home. The batteries were installed in the battery room, and the inverter and charge controller were installed in the north storage area in the home.

When moving wired banks of photovoltaic panels, cover them with sheets of cardboard to prevent them from generating electricity.

The 12 PV panels are mounted in 3 banks of 4 panels each. They are wired in series and parallel to produce an output voltage of over 24 volts. In this case, each panel has an output of about 75 watts. Each bank has its own circuit breaker within the house. This permits any bank to be switched off independently of the others when maintenance is required. It is essential that there be a ventilation airspace, as specified by the manufacturer, below and to the sides of these panels..

This is the photovoltiac electric system installed within the home and shows the conduit and various electrical runs up through the ceiling.

Inverter ⎯⎯

DC charge controller / PV circuit breakers ⎯⎯
DC circuit breakers ⎯⎯
AC circuit breakers ⎯⎯

The sealed battery box has a hinged lid and prevents hydrogen gas from entering the battery room. Hydrogen is released when wet-cell lead-acid batteries are charging. The box vents the gas through a 2" pipe to the roof. A vent at the base of the box brings in fresh air. Some batteries do not outgas hydrogen. Cost is often the determining factor since lead-acid batteries tend to be the least expensive. With proper care, such as checking the water level every month, these lead-acid batteries will last about 5-7 years.

Location of inverter

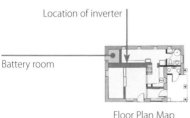

Battery room

Floor Plan Map

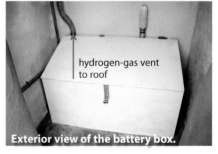

hydrogen-gas vent to roof

Exterior view of the battery box.

Series: A battery or photovoltaic panel connection where the output voltage is the sum of the individual battery or photovoltaic panel voltages.
Parallel: A battery or photovoltaic panel connection where the output current is the sum of the individual battery currents or photovoltaic panel currents.

DVD Location: 1 hour 37 minutes 0 secondss   **Electrical   109**

DC pump for the cistern

DC circulation pump for the radiant floor heat (about 6" tall)

DC wall plug using a 240 volt electrical outlet in order to prevent the plugging in of a 120 volt appliance

The Well Pump

Some research was needed to determine the best well pump to use. Well pumps can draw a lot of power. In addition, many well pumps used for utility-powered homes are 240 volts AC. In a photovoltaic system, this creates complexity because the 120 volt AC electrical system must be converted to 240 volts.

DC pumps are also available. The advantage of DC water pumps is that they do not need to be wired to the inverter, which means that they are slightly more efficient since no power is being lost in the inverter system. If your inverter were ever to break down (which is not common), you would still be able to pump water.

In my desire to keep the electrical equipment as conventional as possible, I ultimately chose to use a 120 volt AC submersible well pump. These can be purchased from the local well-pump suppliers. Many conventionally powered homes use 240 volt well pumps. For a photovoltaic system, this would require additional equipmnent and complicate the system.

Although the depth of this well is 300', the water level in the well is about 35' below the surface. The well pump was placed 25' below the water level. When sizing a pump for your needs, it is the height of your home above the water level in your well that is important, and not the depth to the bottom of the well.

Well Pump Specs:

- ½ horse power, single phase, 120 volt AC
- Draws 9 Amps of power (1,080 watts)
- Averages 11 gallons per minute

Other Options and Considerations

- If possible, place different DC electrical appliances on **separate circuits**. For example, place the DC pump for the cistern on a different circuit breaker than the DC circulation pump for the radiant floor heat. By doing this, you can cut the power to one device for maintenance without affecting the power to the other.

- The positioning of electrical outlets and wall switches is always a problem. Try as you might, it is likely that you will wish you had done something differently. Spend time picturing how you will use the home and where you will need to have a switch. For example, perhaps there should be a light switch at the front door for both the interior light and the exterior porch light. It might be convenient to turn a light on at one side of the room and turn it off where you leave the room. One error I made was not having a switch downstairs for the loft light. It would have been convenient to turn it on and off both from below and from above in the loft.

• Spend the extra money and purchase a true **sine wave inverter**. It will generate the same clean electrical current as comes from the electric company. It eliminates power-generated noise on your television screen, eliminates static on your sound system, and is compatible with all computer and electronic equipment.

• Incorporate a few **DC electrical outlets** in your home. DC light fixtures are available from boating stores and RV stores. If your inverter should need to be sent off for repair, you would still be able to have some lights that run directly off the batteries (in an off-the-grid system).

• Pay careful attention to the size of the **battery room**, particularly if you intend to install the inverter in the same room. The national electrical code has very strict rules on side and front clearances of all electrical components. Since most inverters and charge controllers have LCD monitor panels, you may want this equipment where it can be read inside the home. Remote monitors are also available.

• WIth higher **voltage**, longer electrical runs can be made using thinner and less expensive wiring. For example, if you are using 12 volt photovoltaic panels that are a considerable distance from your batteries, a heavier-gage wire will be needed as compared to that for a 24 volt system. With long DC electrical runs, it may pay to increase the voltage of your system to either 24 or 48 volts.

• If you use a **grid-intertie system**, the grid will be your electrical storage. Some grid-intertie systems also include an on-site battery backup so that the system can keep running for a period of time if the grid goes down. For off-grid systems, the most common backup is a gasoline or natural-gas powered generator. This home does not have a backup system, although a gas generator has been rented on occasion for equalizing the batteries.

• Check the water level of wet-cell **lead-acid batteries** every 4-6 weeks. It is also wise to check the specific gravity of the cells a few times a year. This is done with a device called a hydrometer. If the individual cells of the battery show a wide variation in charge, it is a good idea to rent an AC generator (if one is not part of your system) and equalize the batteries. Equalizing is slightly overcharging all of the batteries in a controlled manner so that all of the battery cells are brought up to a similar rate of charge. Most inverters or charge controllers have a setting for automatically monitoring the equalizing process.

• A **refrigerator** is probably the largest user of electricity in your home. For a photovoltaic-powered home, an energy-efficient refrigerator is mandatory. Look for an Energy Star rated (see page 105) refrigerator. These models save about 15% more power than is required by current federal standards. They also save 40% more energy than the standard model sold in 2001. Buy a refrigerator that is only as large as you need and is the most energy-efficient one that you can afford. For highest efficiency, place your refrigerator out of direct sunlight and leave space between the coils and the walls or cabinets. There are some very energy-efficient DC refrigerators on the market. They tend to be very expensive, costing between $1,000 and $3,000. If you can afford one, they are an excellent choice. For this home, a conventional energy-efficient AC refrigerator was purchased for less than $500 at the local appliance store. With the money saved, an extra $400 photovoltaic panel can be put on the roof to make up for the inefficiency of the AC model as compared to the DC models. I always strived to keep all of the appliances and fixtures in the home as conventional as possible. It is easier to sell the concept of energy efficiency when it does not necessitate investing in an ultra-expensive refrigerator.

Windows and insulation are major factors in weatherizing a house. The windows in this home are double-paned, low-E, and argon-gas filled. It should be noted that the argon will eventually leak out of these windows and no longer add to the insulation value. This is because the home is almost one mile above sea level where the air pressure is less than the gas pressure between the panes. At a lower elevation, the argon does add to the insulation value of the window units.

The low-E coated glass on the south-facing windows results in a small reduction in the winter solar-heat gain through these windows. With the increasing number of warm days caused by global warming, the challenge was to keep this home cool without a mechanical air-conditioning system. The low-E coating also helps to reflect some of the outdoor summer heat, thus maintaining a comfortable indoor temperature.

It is now time to prepare the straw bale, adobe and frame walls for plastering. The ceilings will be covered with wallboard and insulated, and windows will be installed. Anything that will directly contact the earth plaster will also be completed at this time.

All arches over doors and windows were formed with flexible bamboo, rather than with rigid lumber that has been cut and pieced together. The bamboo, when curved and tied together with wire, becomes very strong. Holes were drilled in the adobe to anchor the ends. Partial bales of straw were used as filler on top of the bamboo. An alternative would be to fill the space with straw-clay, which consists of straw with enough mud to bond it together. We used expanded metal lath around some arches and cob (a firm mud-and-straw mix with more mud than straw) on others. The underlying surface must be rigid so that the earth plaster adheres properly. All methods have worked well, and after a few years there has been no cracking of the finished plaster.

The arch to the right is in the kitchen. This opens to the north room.

Expanded metal lath or a natural mesh is added around all windows and doors. Jute is preferable if using earth plaster. All of these materials are affixed to the bales with landscape staples. Any pockets behind the lath are packed with loose straw or straw/clay.

Secured with landscape staples

Nailed to post with washer

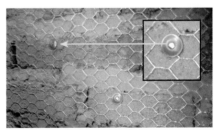

Wire netting is nailed over all the adobe walls. Although not necessary for earth plaster, the stucco netting was wrapped around the walls with a 2-foot overlap at the corners for seismic reinforcement. Some research and shake tests* have shown this to be effective for sesimic zones 3 and above. Although this area is in a relatively safe seismic zone, it seemed like good insurance.

* Shake tests by the Getty Seismic Adobe Project (GSAP) at Stanford University in 1991 and 1995. The research shows inexpensive and minimally invasive techniques for reinforcing adobe structures.

1 Wallboard is used for the ceilings and the frame walls. Wallboard, unlike many of the other finish materials in this home, requires a certain amount of precision in its installation. Since it is a mass-produced material, the machine-made precision surface shows any imperfections at the joints and screw holes if not carefully installed.

Edge of wallboard rests on this face

2x4 nailer boards installed between trusses for securing the wallboard with screws

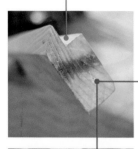

To act as a retainer for the wallboad, a notch was ripped with a table saw into the 2x4s. These were nailed to the bottom of the trusses where they meet the wall. With the sheet supported at the bottom, the installation of the wallboard was much easier. It also made a nicely trimmed transition from the ceiling to the. wall below.

A few narrow sheets of wallboard are left off at the highest point in the ceiling to provide access for blowing insulation above the wallboard. After a section is insulated, the wallboard is installed.

Collar ties consisting of two 2x6s with a 2x spacer were added to the pre-engineered trusses for extra rigidity and for visual interest. The collar ties contain hidden electrical outlets on the top surface for the optional future installation of lights and wall fans. With the wallboard installed, the seams are taped and mudded. Mud, when referring to wallboard, is a white joint compound made specifically for the purpose of hiding seams.

2 Cellulose insulation is manufactured from recycled newspapers with a small amount of borax or boric acid added for flame and insect resistance. It is applied to the depth required for an R-55 rating (at R3.0-3.7 per inch, this is a depth of about 15-18 inches). Since it is being blown in dry, the insulation eventually settles to around R-50. Local code only required insulating to R-30. One advantage of blown-in insulation is that it fills all the cracks and gaps which often remain when typical bat insulation is used.

The problem with the dry-blown cellulose is that it will settle a bit with time, so extra material must be blown in to account for this. Another method would be to hire a professional installer to wet blow the cellulose in place. This method has some advantages, as it is not dusty, will not settle, and stays where it is sprayed. This is particularly helpful when blowing insulation into steeply pitched ceilings because it will not tend to slide down to the lowest point. Corrugated cardboard baffles were added to our insulation space to prevent insulation from accumulating at the base of the pitch. DVD Location: 1 hour 48 minutes 26 seconds

Another ecological do-it-yourself option is to use cotton batting that contains around 85% pre-consumer recycled denim waste. It is rated at R-3.5-3.7 per inch and has a material such as borate added as a flame retardant. This insulation is sold in batts, so care must be taken to install it without any air gaps.

Avoid extruded polystyrene and fiberglass insulation. Polystyrene includes a blowing agent that is damaging to the ozone layer and also contains chemicals that are a health concern. Fiberglass has a high embodied energy, and some of the binders are potentially toxic.

The advantage of blown-in cellulose is that the equipment and materials can be rented locally from home-building supply stores. Although it is quite dusty during installation, it is easy to install. It is essential to wear a proper respirator and eye protection.

By attaching a plastic plumbing elbow to the nozzle, aiming the insulation into cramped spaces and around corners becomes much easier.

3 Loose straw is used to fill gaps between bales when preparing the straw bale surface for earth plaster, lime plaster, or cement stucco. Cracks at the seams between bales can also be filled with a straw-clay mix, which is loose straw with enough mud added to make it stick.

The voids between the framing for the trusses on the gable ends will need to be filled before earth plastering, lime plastering, or stuccoing. Dimensional lumber is commonly wrapped with tar paper to protect it from moisture. Clay-straw can be packed behind stucco netting. A better natural building approach would be to replace the stucco netting with netting made from jute or to fill the spacing between the framing with a straw/clay mix or cob. (See page 119.)

Reed mat, which is sold for sun shades in home-supply stores, is a preferred alternative to expanded metal lath and stucco netting when using earth plaster. This material can be applied to wallboard and OSB-sheeted walls when these surfaces are to be earth plastered.

The Pros and Cons of Stucco Netting

Galvanized stucco netting looks like chicken wire with a slightly heavier gauge. New Mexico code specified that stucco netting be installed on all straw bale surfaces that were to be plastered. This may be reasonable if you are going to use a cement stucco or gypsum plaster finish. However, it is not considered the best practice for an earth plaster finish. The straw bale surface itself is so fibrous that earth plaster bonds to it quite easily. The wet mud surrounds the fibers and creates multiple attachment points. Despite our desire to leave the netting off the straw bales where earth plaster was to be used, we followed state code. If your code permits, apply earth plaster directly to the bales without netting.

Stucco netting, expanded metal lath, or natural netting, is required when bonding stucco or plaster to a non-straw surface. This would be the case when plastering to the vapor barrier around windows and doors and at the top of the walls. Without some sort of mesh, the plaster finish will not stick.

Another disadvantage of stucco netting in day-to-day terms is that it does cut down on the range of wireless internet connections. The signal will go through the walls, but multiple walls can significantly reduce the signal levels. The problem may be compounded with interior adobe walls that contain stucco netting on both sides of the wall. A second range-extending transmitter might be necessary to get an adequate signal across multiple rooms or out to the yard.

Stucco netting   Expanded metal lath

4 Below is one way to seal around windows so that rainwater will not seep into the straw bales. The tar paper is installed starting with layer 1. Keep penetrations to a minimum and away from the window area. Use a high-quality silicone caulk to seal any penetrations and overlaps of the tar paper.

Window detail before the application of mesh over the tar paper

Layer 5: The top layer of tar paper overlaps the side pieces (see yellow outline) and the window nailing flange. Thoroughly caulk all junctions and overlaps with a high-quality silicone caulk.

Layer 4: Window unit. Note the nailing flange around the window. Use plenty of quality silicone caulk on the underside of the flange before nailing.

Layer 3: The side pieces fold around the inside window area and the front face of the 4x4 post, overlapping Layer 2 at the bottom. (Right-side piece is not shown.)

Layer 2: The tar paper is cut to fold over the top of the rough sill and over the front face of the 4x4 posts.

Layer 1: Moisture barrier on top straw bale below window. (See page 97 for a view without the tar paper.)

All sheet metal and moisture barriers overlap the material below them to prevent water from entering at the seams.

Left: Loft window detail after the application of mesh on top of the tar paper. Mesh allows the plaster to stick to the tar paper.

Vapor barrier over wood frame and straw Upper sheets overlap the lower sheets.

Expanded-metal lath (or jute or burlap) on top of tar paper. Thoroughly silicone caulk all nail-penetration areas.

Window unit

1"-deep metal flashing to retain the bottom of the plaster

"L"-shaped sheet-metal splash guard to prevent driving rain from hitting the wall. The sheet metal overlaps the roof.

5 The lower 2' of the exterior wall is a splash guard of stucco or lime plaster. This protects the earth plaster from rain splash-back erosion and provides some pleasing aesthetic possibilities.

1. A string is stretched horizontally to indicate the top of the stucco. Stucco netting is installed with landscape staples, and a 3-coat stucco system is applied.

2-3. The first stucco coat is "scratched" to ensure a good bond of the second coat.

4. When this first coat is dry, a second stucco coat is applied. These stucco coats are applied before the first coat of earth plaster is applied on the wall above. The stucco color coat will be applied before the finish coat of earth plaster.

5. This splash guard continues up to the bottom of the lower windows and prevents rainwater from flowing onto the earth plaster and eroding it. The lower splash guard has worked very well in this high-desert climate. In areas of high annual rainfall, the splash guard would not be necessary, as the entire wall would have to be a more rain-resistant material.

6. In hindsight, lime plaster would have been used instead of cement stucco. This could be lime plaster applied directly to the straw or a thinner coat on top of the mud. Lime, being a more breathable material than stucco, is better at allowing moisture within the wall to evaporate out. Lime plaster is tinted with powered pigments and will weather to a nice patina. When fully cured, it turns into calcium carbonate which is very hard. *(Stephen Bennett applying pigmented lime wash in Corrales, NM. Photo: Kelly Cozart)*

Under roof orerhang   Exposed to direct rain

Above: After a few years of exposure to direct rain, the junction of the earth plaster to stucco on the west wall has eroded a bit.. This was partially due to installing the stucco with a moderately-beveled top to keep water flowing outward.. This caused the earth plaster to erode at the thinner outside edge. Overall, the smooth finish of the earth plaster has held up well because of the wheat paste which was added to the earth plaster. (See page 121.)

Earth Plaster

45° bevel of spalsh guard   Splash Guard   Minimal bevel of spalsh guard

Other Details

Right: Straw/clay is made from loose straw that is mixed with enough mud to make it stick together. Cob is similar except it has a lot more mud to make it thick and sticky. Both materials can be used for filling voids.

Below: To attach this coat hook to an adobe wall, expanded metal lath was screwed to the back. Nails with washers were then used to affix the unit to the wall. A coat of plaster will hide the lath and make a very stout bond to the wall. (See page 125.)

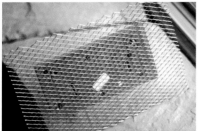

The cement mortar is raked to permit easier leveling of the flagstone.

Left: About 3" of cement mortar was used as a base for the flagstone window seats. The cement provides a firm base which can bear considerable weight. In addition, the earth plastering workshop was to start in two days, and a mud base would not have dried in time.

Below left and right: The space below this window (see page 97) was filled with cob. It was then decided to cut a slab out of the cob in order to form a small nicho for books and magazines below the planned flagstone shelf. The finished result can be seen on page 15.

10. Earth Plaster

Mud is one of the oldest building materials and is used around the world. When clay and sand are mixed in the proper proportion, a durable, hard, and beautiful earth plaster is created. This natural material makes a moisture-permeable protective surface for both straw bale and adobe. Earth plaster's ability to wick moisture away from the straw makes it one of the best materials for a protective finish. Cement stucco, on the other hand, can tend to trap moisture within the bales. Mud also has the lowest embodied energy (defined on page 14) of any plaster available. Cement stucco and most forms of lime plaster take a considerable amount of energy to manufacture. With a proper mud mix and a sufficiently wide roof overhang, an earth plaster exterior wall finish will last for many years without maintenance. Interior wall finishes may be maintenance free for decades.

Earth plasters can be obtained in several ways. Sometimes they can be dug directly from the work-site soil if it happens to have the proper proportion of sand to clay. Pure clay can also be dug from the ground and mixed with sand, or clay and sand can be purchased separately in bulk, delivered by truck to the work site, and then mixed together. We purchased a sand/clay premix from the local adobe yard. This was the same earth used there for making adobe blocks.

If earth plaster is not a viable option in your area, lime plaster may be appropriate. If necessary, cement stucco could also be used on the exterior. For interior walls, gypsum plaster or lime plaster are beautiful options— either as finish coats or as the entire covering.

This home used a 3-coat earth plaster system. The total thickness ranged from 1" to 1½" depending on the irregularities of the straw bale wall. The purpose of the first two coats was to create an even surface. The key ingredient for a durable, earth plaster finish is wallpaper wheat paste. This environmentally sound powder acts as a binder for the mud and also dramatically increases the resistance of the earth plaster to rain. In addition, wheat paste helps prevent the plaster from "dusting" (the transfer of powder to your hand when touched). When properly mixed, earth plasters are hard and crack resistant. Surface finishes range from smooth to textured. Depending on the clay used, the color may vary widely.

An advantage of working with earth plaster is that it does not have the short setup time of gypsum plaster and therefore can be worked for hours. Gypsum plaster and cement stucco undergo a chemical reaction while curing and, once set, the material can no longer be worked. It is therefore essential that all surface smoothing be finished within the limited time period.

A two-day workshop was held for the initial coats of earth plaster. Like the straw bale workshop, this again provided us with free manual labor while the volunteers acquired knowledge for their own future projects.

The color of earth plaster will vary depending on the type of clay and sand that is used.

The earth plaster recipe below is a starting point. Your mix may vary depending on the chosen clay, the weather conditions, the moisture content of the sand and clay, and how the plaster is to be used. The proportions shown here are for mixing in a large commercial plaster mixer. Mixers can be rented from construction-equipment rental centers.

- **Approximately 70% sand and 30% clay**
    (about 18 shovelfuls of the pre mix in a large commercial mixer)
- **1/2 to 3/4 pounds of dry wallpaper wheat paste**
- **4 large handfuls of chopped straw**
- **Thoroughly dry mix all materials**
- **Add water to produce the proper consistency**

Wheat paste: For many decades, wheat paste was used to glue wallpaper to walls. It is a powdered, non-toxic glue made from wheat starch. In the past few years, wheat paste has become more difficult to find in local stores. It may be easiest to order wheat paste in bulk over the internet.
Visit www.BuildingWithAwareness.com and click on *Resources* for a list of suppliers.

1 A premix was delivered from the local adobe yard. It consisted of the approximate proportions of 70% sand to 30% clay. If you are mixing your own sand and clay from scratch, these ingredients must be mixed while dry.

2 The premix contained small stones and gravel that had to be sifted out through ⅛" hardware cloth (a coarse metal screen). The dirt was shoveled onto the screen and then pushed around by hand. This step might also be necessary if using local soil.

3 The result was a stone-free sand/clay mix (left picture) that sifted through the screen. The pea-sized stones to the far right were what remained on top of the screen. Even these can be put to good use. We used them as a gravel surface for walkways around the home.

4 We put 18 shovelfuls of the premix into a running large commercial mixer. Your amount may vary depending on the capacity of the mixer you use. For the initial coats, it is worth the cost and effort to rent one of these mixers, as you want to generate a continuous supply for the plasterers.

5 Four large handfuls of chopped straw are then added to the dry mix. If you do not have access to a mulcher (see page 135), you can cut the straw off the bales with a chain saw. We used loose straw collected from the ground while stacking the bales.

6 For the size of our mixer we added about ¾ of a pound of dry wallpaper wheat paste. The mixer should run until all of the dry ingredients are thoroughly homogenized. Only then is water added. If water is added too soon, or if the wheat paste is added to a wet mix of mud, clumps will form and show up as white spots on your wall (photo to right). Thorough dry mixing will prevent this from happening.

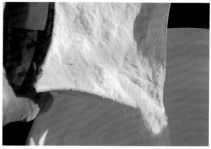

7 Water is added until the mud achieves the consistency of chocolate mousse. This will permit the mud to properly adhere to the straw. If you count the number of buckets of water added, you will know the proper amount to use in subsequent mixes.

8 The mud is placed on a hawk and then transferred to the straw using an upward movement of the trowel. It may help to shimmy the trowel back and forth to force the mud firmly into the fibers of the straw.

9 Smoothing corners takes a bit of practice. The mud is transferred from the trowel to the wall with a diagonal sweep. The trailing edge of the trowel should be firmly pressed into the wall. The leading edge is held away from the wall. Multiple passes of the trowel will smooth out the mud.

10 As the mud becomes firm, another coat can be applied. If the previous coat has dried out, lightly spray it with water so that the next coat will bond properly. Unlike cement stucco, it is not necessary to scratch the first coat of earth plaster. The mud will stick and bond to itself.

Ultimately, you may end up with an inch of mud on the walls and sometimes more depending on the undulations of the straw bales and the thickness desired for durability.

In the kitchen, the straw bale wall transitions into a wood frame wall with wallboard. The wall-board was coated with a commercially available sealer to prevent moisture absorption. Expanded metal lath covers the junction of the earth plaster on straw to the wallboard. Reed mat (**DVD Location: 2 hours 10 minutes 53 seconds**) nailed over the wallboard would have been a better choice for mud plaster. The metal lath on the wallboard is suspended about ¼" off the surface using special nails with fiber washers. The earth plaster is then applied to the entire wall. Ultimately, a ¼" skim coat of gypsum plaster is applied in the kitchen as a finish coat of greater durability. Gypsum plaster cannot be used where it will be in direct contact with water, such as around showers.

Above Left and Center: Prior to plastering an adobe wall, the corners can be rounded with a file made by wrapping expanded metal lath around a 2x4. **Above Right:** The wall containing the coat rack (as installed on page 119) is given a coat of plaster. This adobe wall is in the entry of the home.

When the mud is applied in very thick coats and dries quickly under the sun, it is likely that some minor cracks will form. The finish coat of earth plaster will fill these without a problem.

A pool trowel (with rounded ends) and a finishing trowel are both good for applying mud to large surfaces. Although more expensive, stainless steel trowels are best because they do not rust.

Tips

When plastering indoors, the rooms must be well ventilated in order to remove the many gallons of water that will evaporate from the plaster. Otherwise, this moisture may condense on the ceilings and cause problems.

Do not plaster outdoors if the temperature is expected to drop below freezing. Plaster that freezes right after application will lose its structural integrity and will have to be scraped off and reapplied. If there is a chance the temperature may drop just a bit below freezing, tarps can be hung around the structure to contain the heat.

Electrical boxes are covered with masking tape prior to plastering. It is very easy to bury outlets during the frenzy of slapping mud on the walls. Placing a long screw in the receptacle's screw hole will aid in finding the box behind the mud.

The west living room wall, the kitchen, and part of the bathroom were given a ¼" skim coat of gypsum plaster. This was applied as a finish coat on top of the first two coats of earth plaster. The gypsum plaster was mixed with some masonry sand and applied in a single day, working from the top of this wall to the bottom. Unlike earth plaster, you cannot take a break with gypsum plaster. The gypsum bonded very well to the mud and is still free of cracks several years later.
DVD Location: 2 hours 15 minutes 48 seconds

11. FINISH WORK

inish work encompasses a wide range of tasks. The final coat of earth plaster will be the finishing touch on the home, so anything that adjoins the walls—such as shelving, baseboard tile, cabinet frames, etc.—must all be completed at this time. This is also a creative phase of construction in that many aesthetic decisions are made regarding color and detailing. These processes can also take a considerable amount of time. We not only built the house but also made most of the doors, installed all of the trim tile, built the sink counters, and made the bamboo door pulls for the cabinets. When people ask why it takes so long to build your own home, the answer may be in the details. In the end, they are worth the extra effort.

Shelving is made from scrap 2x lumber, and salvaged tile is used around the kitchen counter. Reflector-type metal light fixtures were retrofitted to a track-light system and focus the light to the countertops.

The bathroom was given a skim coat of **gypsum plaster**, except in the shower area. Powdered natural pigments were added to the wet plaster mix. When dry, two coats of sealer were applied. Do not use gypsum plaster around tubs and showers, as gypsum plaster will not hold up to constant dampness. The "truth window," showing the straw bale construction, was made from a porthole off a friend's sailboat.

1. Non-VOC paints should definitely be used. VOC's create ground level ozone and smog. In addition, they contribute to indoor air pollution. Many of the large paint companies are now manufacturing non-VOC paints, as are smaller companies.

2. Shellac was used on all wooden floors. Shellac, combined with a good wax, makes an excellent protective surface that is environmentally sound. (Also see page 25.)

The third and final **color coat** was added to the exterior, cement-stucco splash guard (pages 23 and 118). Wet down the previous coat and work from wall corner to wall corner in one application to prevent visible seams. If using lime plaster instead of stucco, this would be a color lime coat or wash.

Acid stains can be used to create concrete floors that are rich in color. The stains which are specifically made for this purpose work by chemically reacting with materials in the concrete. We used 4 different colors consisting of light tan, reddish-brown, green, and a very diluted black. The application was done with a hand-pressurized sprayer. Sometimes we just poured small amounts of acid stains on the floor. The coloring was approached as in a watercolor, often letting one color flow into the next. (Also see page 42.)

Ferrous Sulfate—A Greener Alternative To Coloring Concrete: Care must be taken when working with acid stains and the leftover residue. Ferrous sulfate is an iron fertilizer supplement that is used in agriculture. It is ecologically sound in that it is essentially rust. It can be applied when the concrete is still curing and can also be used on older floors. The material can be mixed with water and sprayed on or applied with a mop. The floor can also be wet down with a hose and the ferrous sulfate sprinkled on dry. Experiment before committing to the entire floor. A mottled earth-toned patina is the result, and the color ranges from yellow ochre to reddish brown.

 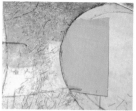 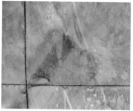

Above Left: Pieces of straw are used to create uneven drying of the acid stain. Plastic bags, newspaper, leaves, and old rags can all be used for this purpose. Let one coat dry before applying the second. **Center:** A piece of cardboard is used to mask a section of concrete where color is not desired. **Right:** After the two coats of acid stain have dried, a residue is left that must be cleaned up with water. We used a wet/dry vacuum to take up the water and residue. The color will darken considerably when the floor is waxed, so keep this in mind before applying more than two coats.

Placing a decorative tile: This old Mexican tile had been in the family for many years. **1.** A section of adobe wall was chiseled down about 1/4" to allow for the tile thickness. Expanded metal lath was nailed in place. **2.** Tile mortar was worked into the metal lath, and the tile was carefully positioned. **3.** Once dry, gaps were filled with earth plaster. The completed tile is shown on page 127.

Raised Floor: The wood floor was made two steps higher than the concrete floor. This Japanese-style technique of defining room areas is very effective in small homes. A 2x6 frame was constructed, covered with a ¼" plywood base and then finished with salvaged oak. The oak had been painted black in its previous life. By flipping the oak over and sanding the unpainted surface, an attractive floor was obtained with less work. It was then given 2 coats of shellac and a coat of wax. **DVD Location:** 2 hours 14 min 45 seconds

Top: Bamboo was used for the loft railing. Scrap pieces of copper pipe held the bamboo in place. **Upper Left:** When house construction first started, a trip was made to the local salvage yard where a variety of 2x12s were purchased. These were used for scaffolding during construction. When the house was completed, they were cut up and turned into this bookcase in the main room. **Upper Right:** The cabinets in the loft were roughly framed in with 2x lumber. The greenish finish is a low-VOC stain. Trim was added around the openings and various colored paint combinations were tried. Reed mats fill the center of the removable doors. **Lower Left:** Scrap lumber from the framing was used for the kitchen shelving. Before gluing up the shelves, the curve of the end-grain was alternated in order to prevent warping.

Upper Left: Bamboo pulls were made for the cabinet doors. **Above:** When the interior walls are finished with earth plaster, it is important to include baseboard tile so that the floors can be mopped without damaging the plaster on the walls. Slate was used for this purpose. **Left:** The scoring in the floor was filled with grout, and the entire floor was given a coat of wax. **Below:** This is the completed kitchen, looking south. The black cast-in-place concrete counters receive direct sunlight in the winter and add to the thermal mass.

This ¼"-thick layer of earth plaster will complete the home. If you are using lime plaster, gypsum plaster or stucco, this step will be the color coat. One advantage of a three-coat earth plaster system is that, by the time you get to the finish coat, you will be quite proficient at plastering. It is a very forgiving medium, and the hours of work have not only made you skilled at smoothing mud, but you have also been able to cancel your gym membership, thanks to the upper-body workout.

Earth plasters have a beautiful tonal range of colors, which will eliminate the need and cost of paints. Colors range from the traditional brown tones to a creamy white. By adding natural powdered pigments to the mix, a full range of hues are possible.

In this project, the natural hue of the brown mud will give color to the exterior walls. This exterior finish coat is usually soupier (contains more water) than the first two coats. With a wetter mix, it is easier to level out the plaster and bring it to the desired smoothness. Since this final coat is a thin layer, it will follow the contours of the earlier coats of mud. Any irregularities in the overall surface should have been addressed in the previous layers. Our interior walls used both brown mud and white mud. The white mud was a thicker mix than what was used for the exterior coat. The amount of water depends on the type of sand and clay used and on the feel of the mix when applying test patches.

The finish coats of earth plaster demonstrated here were all mixed on site. Pre-mixed clay-based plasters for indoor use are also available. Companies, such as American Clay —The Original Earth Plaster®, offer finish earth plasters in a wide variety of colors. This can greatly speed up the process by eliminating the time needed to custom mix materials and pigments.

Finding the clay

While white may seem like an unlikely color for mud, it is actually quite common. You see it everyday in ceramic dishware. This is the same material that potters use in making ceramic pots. White clay is available from ceramic supply stores. Most of the material is sold in 50-pound sacks. The clay that we used was white Kaolin "tile 6" clay. It was a good choice because it does not tend to crack with age. (See page 120 for more places to find clay.)

Sand

White sand is also available from ceramic supply stores in a variety of grits, including 30, 60, 70, and even 90. The higher the number, the finer the sand. It helps to mix multiple grits together, as the different sizes of sand grains tend to pack together more tightly and form a harder surface. Ordinary mortar sand can also be used if it is sifted through a screen. Mortar sand will change the color and texture, so first make a test mix to see the results. Always wear the appropriate dust mask or respirator when working with sand. You do not want to inhale any of the dust while the sand is in a dry state.

Wheat Paste

If you will be doing more than just a single wall with earth plaster, it will be substantially less expensive to purchase the wheat paste in bulk. Logon to www.buildingwithawareness.com and click on Resources to find current mail-order firms. When buying 10 pounds or more, we usually paid less than $3.00 per pound. (See page 121 for more information.)

Finish plaster mix

Depending on the clay and sand that you are using, the actual mix will vary. Only test patches will allow you to fine-tune the proportions of the dry ingredients and water. We used the mix shown below:

Ingredients for a small electric cement mixer:

60% sand consisting of both 60 and 70 grit
40% white Kaolin clay (in powder form)
2-3 handfuls of finely chopped straw (add or reduce as desired)
1½-2 cups of powdered wheat paste
water

A test patch showing the color, texture, and durability when rubbed after it is dry

A pool trowel and a finishing trowel for applying mud in large areas

A selection of smaller Japanese finishing trowels

For fine polishing, a yogurt lid or a smooth stone can be used as an alternative to a trowel.

1 Start by placing your materials near the cement mixer for easy access. The 50-pound bags to the left contain white silica sand. The bags to the right contain the white Kaolin clay. Until the clay is needed, store it in a dry place to prevent lumps from forming due to moisture in the air. Wear an appropriate dust mask during the entire mixing process

2 The loose straw is run through an electric mulcher two times in order to create finer pieces of straw. This particular mulcher features a plastic bag retainer on the bottom that collects the chopped straw. Store the chopped straw in bags so that it stays dry until needed.

DVD Location: 2 hours 20 min 50 seconds

3 A small bucket can be used to accurately measure the proper proportion of sand to clay. This ensures consistent results from batch to batch. In this particular mix, the ratio is 60% sand to 40% clay. We added 6 buckets of sand to the mixer. To reduce dust, keep the mixer off while adding dry ingredients.

Electric mulcher: A small portable device that uses a spinning mono-filament plastic line to chop leaves and other gardening debris. It is essentially a weed trimmer on legs. The straw can be cut manually if you do not have access to such a device.

4 Next we added 4 buckets of clay to the mixer. The clay can tend to dry out your hands, so gloves will help protect them.

5 Throw in a few handfuls of finely chopped straw. The amount is determined by your aesthetic preference. In this case, we added about 4 handfuls. You may choose to add more or none at all.

6 We added about 1½ to 2 cups of powdered wheat paste. This amount will vary depending on the quantity of the mix. The wheat paste acts as a binder to prevent dusting (powder that sticks to your hand when rubbing a dry wall) and to make the earth plaster mix more water-resistant.

Powdered natural pigments can also be added to the plaster to create a wide range of colors. Some possible additives include mica for a slight sparkle, iron oxide, and yellow ochre.

7 The mixer is now turned on, and the dry ingredients should tumble until thoroughly mixed. It is essential to dry mix all of the ingredients before water is added. Adding water too early will result in an uneven mix. Continue to wear your protective gear.

8 Water is slowly added with a garden hose or bucket while the mixer continues to rotate. Go slowly at this point. You can always add more water, but you cannot take it away if the mix becomes too wet. Stop the mixer occasionally and check to see that the ingredients in the back of the drum are getting wet. If necessary, while the mixer off, use a small shovel or trowel to loosen any dry material stuck to the sides.

9 Continue to mix and adjust the water content until you have a consistency that is similar to chocolate mousse. The plaster will stick to your hands and hold peaks similar to whipped cream. Now remove the plaster from the mixer and load it into a wheelbarrow or bucket. Wash out the mixer to be ready for the next load. Premix as many loads as you will need for the wall section to be plastered.

Application techniques are best seen in the video. The first step is to spray down the previous layer of mud. Apply the plaster with a trowel and smooth it out to a consistent depth. Smaller tools are used to work around wall details, such as this window shelf.

Left: A yogurt lid is used to apply mud to the inside curves of the nicho. Plastic wrap is used to smooth out convex curves (see the DVD). When the plaster becomes firm, switch to a finishing trowel or a yogurt lid for buffing and final smoothing.

The end result of the two-toned wall in the living area: The flagstone makes a nice division between the two colors. Color pigments can also be added to white earth plaster to achieve a variety of tones. (See page 15 for another view of this wall.)

The exterior finish coat is much soupier than the white plaster to the right. The only difference is the amount of water used, which was determined by the feel of the plaster. The white plaster had a creamier texture, and the brown mud was grittier.

Above: For the exterior finish coat, it helps to have at least two people working on a particular wall. After spraying the surface with water, one person applies the initial coat of earth plaster, and the second person follows up with the final smoothing. For the exterior walls, a pool trowel can be used for working the surface to the desired finish. As the mud sets, it will become leather like, and the trowel will make a "twang" sound as it is worked. At this stage, apply firmer pressure.

Corners can be worked to sharp edges as shown here on an adobe wall, or the corners can be bullnosed. This plaster, as can be seen by the wet sheen, is still pliable and not ready for the final smoothing. As the mud hardens, a pool trowel can be used with broad sweeping strokes to slowly work out the trowel marks as desired. The photo to the right shows the mud changing color as it dries. Most earth plasters will lighten as they dry.

Scaffolding is needed for all plaster work. Use what is necessary to get the job done safely. Scaffolding can also be rented.

There are two questions that are always asked regarding this home. One is, "How much did it cost?" The total cost was about $88,000, not including the land. This did include the entire photovoltaic electrical system, the cistern, high-end windows, and everything else that has been shown in this book and in the DVD video. Costs vary greatly from region to region and also depend on how much of the work you do yourself. Your cost for a similar project could vary tremendously. For a complete cost breakdown of this home, please visit www.BuildingWithAwareness.com and click on *Cost*.

The other question is, "What would you do differently the next time?" All design decisions such as the passive heating and cooling, thermal mass, and the layout of the home have worked beautifully and as predicted. The home stays very comfortable the year round and is a pleasure to live in—both functionally and aesthetically. As with any construction project, there are always some elements that would be handled differently the next time. Some have been indicated throughout this book. Tips and additional notes are included here. These comments may seem obvious to some. They are added just as a reminder.

Saving Money

When possible, buy from businesses that cater to the professional construction trade. They are listed in the phone book and are not generally open to the public. Tell them that you are building your own home and are working as your own contractor. Sometimes you will need to set up an account. You may be able to save up to 50% on various plumbing parts, as compared to buying from the home-supply chains. Many tools that are of higher quality and yet the same or lower cost can also be purchased from the above businesses. The most common tools in these categories are hand tools, wheelbarrows, etc.

Design

Never rush the design phase of your home. A poorly designed home cannot be fixed with even the best craftsmanship. Spend time on paper sketches, ideas, and drawings before you spend time building the home.

The tankless hot water heater is to the left, and the pressure tank for the well is to the right.

Mechanical Room

Problems:

The gas heating appliances used a conventional flue. Because of this, code required that two fresh air vents be cut in the door or wall to supply combustion air. This is like having an open window in the room and causes heat loss in the winter. If an appliance uses room air for combustion, the exhaust is vented to the outside, and cold air is drawn into the room to replace the exhaust air. Hot-water heaters for both the radiant heating and fresh-water heating are then less efficient since they are housed in a cold environment. There is also the potential for pipes to freeze if the outside temperature drops low enough. It is essential to insulate both the hot and cold water pipes in a mechanical room which has vents to outside air. The room can get down to 45° F when the outside temperature is in the teens. When the mechanical room is cold, the bathroom loses some heat as well since it shares a frame wall with the mechanical room (see page 81). The slab in the mechanical room is continuous with the bathroom floor, thus making the bathroom floor colder. A thermal break in the floor would have helped to prevent this. In the winter, the pressure-tank water also gets very cold. The colder the water, the more energy is needed to heat it for sinks and showers.

Tips and Solutions:

1. Use a direct-vent instantaneous (also known as tankless) water heater with a pilotless ignition. This provides an additional energy savings of about 20%. Direct-vent units draw combustion air through a pipe from the outside, thus keeping cold air out of the room itself. The combustion air is totally separated from the room air. Mentally approach the design of the mechanical room as if it were part of the living space of the home.

2. Insulate the mechanical room door or purchase an insulated door to prevent heat loss.

3. There is a tendency to make mechanical rooms as small as possible in order to conserve space and cost. This is not always the best policy. At some point in the future, you will need either to replace an appliance or work on the plumbing. Make the room a bit larger than the absolute minimum size. You will thank yourself the next time you have to replace a leaky valve.

4. Always check with your local code official, installer, or gas utility to ensure that you are complying with code and the specifications of the appliance.

Radiant Floor Heating

Problem: Using a conventional tank hot-water heater for a home under 1,500 square feet is sometimes done to save money. This is not cost efficient in the long run. Conventional hot-water heaters for radiant heating have the same problems as they do for heating domestic water. They keep the water hot 24 hours per day whether it is needed or not. Water is heated even when the circulation pump is not on which, in a well-insulated home such as this, is quite common. Therefore energy and money are wasted. These are called "standby losses," which is heat lost through the tank itself and the water pipes. The loss is due to the temperature differences between the tank and pipes and the surrounding air.

Solution: Use an instantaneous hot-water heater (models are available for this purpose) or a high-efficiency boiler for the radiant system. These will heat the water only when the hydronic heating circulation pump is on. If you must use a conventional HW heater for the floor heat, at least buy a sealed combustion unit and add an insulation blanket to the tank.

Battery Room Essentials Checklist

1. Heat and insulate the battery room. Lead-acid batteries lose capacity when cold. Also insulate any door which opens to the outdoors. This keeps the room warmer in the winter and helps prevent overheating in the summer. Remember that ventilation is still required for the battery box for proper venting of battery gasses (see page 109) if you are using wet-cell lead-acid batteries.
2. It is a good idea to build the battery box slightly larger than needed to house the batteries that you are currently using. This will permit you to change brands or type, if necessary, when they must be replaced.

Skylights

Benefits: They permit natural lighting which conserves electricity. They also provide a view of the sky and allow the pleasant sound of rain to be heard within the home. Some skylights open for the purpose of venting hot air.

Problems: Skylights lose a tremendous amount of heat in the winter. Cold air can literally drop down from the skylight and feel as if a fan is pushing it. If facing south, the home could overheat in the summer without proper shading of the skylight. The two skylights in this home face north and provide a nice quality of light. The structure was intended to be used as an artist's studio in the future, so north light was important.

Solutions: **1.** Keep skylights to an absolute minimum and use the most efficient units available. Like windows, they can be purchased with various coatings and layers of glass. You may also eliminate skylights and use carefully positioned windows in the wall instead. A window will lose less heat than a skylight.

2. Removable or hinged insulation panels on skylights are essential during the winter months in cold areas. The insulation panels in this home are 3"-thick rigid foam.

3. Use reflective tube-type skylights. These 10"-or-so-diameter compact units bring in light and have a minimal surface area which reduces heat loss and gain.

4. If using conventional window-type skylights, keep them as small as possible and position them so one side of the skylight well is flush with the wall. This will help reflect a soft light into the room. (See photo above and on page 126 at the bottom.)

5. Insulate with foam in the framing around skylight wells. This will reduce heat loss in the winter and heat gain in the summer.

Bathroom

We poured the shower pan before installing the radiant-floor-heat tubing. This reduced the amount of this tubing in the room, and therefore the room is less warm during cold weather, especially since it is on the north side of the home. In hindsight, additional tubing could have been added to the bathroom floor to compensate for its lack in the shower floor.

Increasing Mechanical Ventilation Efficiency:

When air is vented to the outside by the electric bathroom vent fan, fresh outside air is brought into the home to replace it. This enters through cracks and any unsealed areas of the home. This drains heat from the home when the outside temperature is cold and removes cool air when the outside temperature is hot. The solution is to use mechanical heat exchangers in the venting system. In the winter, these compact units warm up the cold outside air as it enters the home through the outside vent, using the warm outward-bound indoor air.

Solar Hot Water

If you do not install a solar hot water system during construction, pre plumb the mechanical room for adding one later. You may also want to make the mechanical room large enough to hold any additional equipment for a solar hot water system (such as a heat exchanger tank). This home is plumbed for a solar hot-water system.

Foundation/slab

Where the foundation grade beam and the interior floor slab meet, the grout cracks due to the different thermal expansion rates of the unheated foundation and the heated and warmer floor slab. This can be avoided by using a flexible floor grout in this area.

Roof Insulation

Consider adding a radiant-heat barrier in addition to the insulation. A radiant-heat barrier looks like aluminum foil. Heat, just like light, is reflected off shiny surfaces. These barriers sometimes require an air space between the reflective surface and the insulation. If the shiny side faces towards the rooms, heat will be reflected back towards the room. Conversely, if it faces the roof, summer heat will be reflected back to the roof.

Plumbing

General information if using small pumps for your water-supply system:
• If using a small pressure pump for your water supply (as opposed to city water or a powerful well pump), 90° bends in the pipes create more friction when water moves through. Using two 45° elbows to turn a corner is better than one 90° bend. Flexible tubing is also a good alternative.
• Use waterless urinals. The use of drinkable water to flush a waste liquid is not ecologically wise.
• Smaller diameter pipes have more friction than larger diameter pipes. As pipes age, they may acquire mineral deposits on the inside, thus further reducing the diameter. A wider pipe may last somewhat longer. However, the downside is that the pipe now has to move more cold water out of the line before the hot water reaches the shower head. Thus more water and energy go down the drain. A half-inch pipe (or the narrowest permitted by code) is better for energy efficiency in hot-water lines.

Electrical

• IMPORTANT: When mounting PV panels to the roof of your home, it is essential that you follow the manufacturer's instructions for the proper air space below the panels. Depending on the type of photovoltaic panels used, insufficient space may cause heat damage to the panels in hot climates.

• When installing the wiring from the PV panels to your charge controller, make sure there is room in the conduit for adding additional wiring later on in case you decide to add more PV panels. Better yet, install the additional cable during construction, or increase the size of the wiring so that it can carry the load of additional panels.

Windows
Buy the best and most energy-efficient windows that you can afford. Insulating blinds can also dramatically improve the comfort of the home by preventing heat loss and gain.

Salvaged Wood
Use salvaged wood whenever possible to prevent the cutting of new wood. This is particularly important in larger dimensional beams and posts that must be cut from older-growth trees. The downside of salvaged wood is that it may not be available the day you need it. Start looking for this wood before you start construction. Depending on the salvage yard, the wood may not be immediately ready to use, as it may contain nails, screws, and blemishes. For our project, this was particularly true for the oak planks used on the raised floor.

Thermal Mass
This home incorporates more thermal mass than is necessary for a successful passive solar home. This was an experiment in maximizing the amount of mass for passive cooling. It was also done for aesthetic reasons and for demonstrating how to construct very thick earthen walls. Although debatable, it is the opinion of some, including myself, that greater amounts of thermal mass help keep the house cooler during the summer months. In this small home, the extra cost of thicker walls was not significant. For your home, 14" or 10" adobe walls should work well. This also has the benefit of increasing indoor floor space without increasing the total square footage of the home. Remember that it is more effective to have lots of exposed square footage of 4"-thick thermal mass than a minimal amount of 10"-thick mass walls.

Working With Contractors
• When building your own home, there are many decisions to be made. At times, it is easy to drop your guard and assume that, when hiring a contractor with a particular skill such as plumbing or electricity, the "pros" will make the right decisions. This is not always the case as we learned with the combustion air venting in our mechanical room. It is not necessarily a failing of the contractors, as they may not realize that you are striving for maximum efficiency, and they may not be familiar with the best methods for that. Even though the installation they favor meets code, it may not be the most appropriate option for an energy-efficient solar home.
• Always try to select contractors by getting recommendations from others. Tell the contractors that you are striving for maximum energy efficiency and ask them what they would recommend. This is where it helps to educate yourself first, so you can make the wisest decisions.

Vaulted Ceilings
This small home has vaulted ceilings to make the main room feel larger. Vaulted ceilings can create winter heating problems in that warm air rises, thus making the living area cooler. The thermal mass and radiant floor heat help to compensate for this. Most importantly, this home is so small that it was decided to use a vaulted ceiling to gain loft space. This saved money by eliminating the need to build an additional room. Because of heat loss, vaulted ceilings can be problematic in any home and particularly in larger homes.

Pace Yourself
Building your own home can, at times, be stressful and tiring. There is always a feeling that the construction is moving slower than it should and that your bank account is shrinking faster than it should. Remember to take breaks—or even a week off now and then. The process can be both fun and creative. Look at your home construction project as if it were a piece of art.

A Condensed Overview Of Features Of This Home

Square Footage: The house was designed to be no larger than needed. The small size allowed money to be put into details and aesthetics, instead of more square footage. A small house also requires less energy for heating and cooling and therefore costs less to run from month to month. Although this is a very compact house, the same basics can be scaled to any size structure. **Passive Heating:** The long south side of the house contains the majority of the windows for solar heat gain in the winter. A minimum amount of window area is on the north side to reduce winter heat loss. Thick thermal mass walls passively absorb heat during the day and release the stored heat back into the rooms at night. **Backup Heating:** Some sort of backup heating was required by code. We used hydronic radiant floor heating. **Passive Cooling:** To take advantage of the local climate with its hot summer days and cool nights, high and low windows are opened at night to cool down the thermal mass walls and are closed during the day. The roof overhang on the south side is designed to prevent direct sunlight from entering the home in the summer. Windows facing west are kept to a minimum to prevent heat gain in the late afternoon. **Utilities:** Natural gas is used for the cooking range and oven, the radiant floor heat, and a tankless hot-water heater. **Electricity:** All electrical power is 100% photovoltaic (PV) generated from sunlight. The PV panels are rated 900 watts at 24 volts DC. A battery bank which consists of twelve L-16 batteries, is wired to provide 1,050 amp-hours of storage capacity at 24 volts DC. A sine wave inverter converts 24 volts DC to 120 volts AC and has a maximum power output of 4,000 watts. All appliances are AC and were chosen for their high energy-efficiency ratings. All lights are compact fluorescent. **Foundation:** Over 7% of all greenhouse gasses comes from the production of cement. A rubble trench foundation was used to reduce the amount of cement in the foundation by over 50%, as compared to a conventional foundation. **Wood:** Any wood beams over 6" square consist of salvaged lumber in order to make the cutting of old-growth trees unnecessary. Wood floors are made of either recycled oak or of aspen. (Aspen is a fast-growing alternative to pine.) **Wall Construction:** 4x4 wood posts support a 4x8 beam. Posts are spaced up to 8' apart and have two-string straw bales for wall infill. The insulation value is approximately R-30 to R-35 (with plaster on the inside and outside). The interior walls consist of one 2'-thick adobe main thermal-mass wall and 10"-thick adobe secondary walls. The plumbing walls are of wood-frame construction. **Wall Finishes:** Plaster for the interior and exterior walls is an earth plaster mixture. Gypsum Plaster: In areas where more durability is needed, such as in the kitchen, a ¼" finish coat of gypsum plaster was applied on top of the mud in lieu of a final coat of earth plaster. This gypsum plaster was left unpainted. **Floor:** The floor is 4" concrete (acid-stained) with hydronic heating tubes. This exposed concrete floor adds to the thermal mass needed for passive solar heating. **Roof Insulation:** The roof has a minimum of R-55 cellulose insulation. The dry-blown cellulose will settle to approximately R-50. Cellulose is made from recycled newspaper. **Windows:** Double-paned, low-E glass was used throughout the house. **Cistern:** This is a 1,500 gallon polyethylene tank which stores the rainwater used for flushing the toilet, for the cold water in the washing machine, and for a gardening spigot.

For more information and tips on green building, please visit our web site at:
www.BuildingWithAwareness.com

Acknowledgements

Putting together a DVD video and a book is a massive effort that could only have been accomplished with the help of many people. I would particularly like to thank Peggy Owens and Al Owens for their diligence and expertise in all areas from copy editing and proof reading to construction; Emily Dahmen for compiling the index, proofreading, and composing the music for the video; Chris Plant at New Society Publishers for taking a chance with the *Building With Awareness* DVD; Kelly Cozart for scanning hundreds of slides for the book; and Paula Eastwood for pre-press assistance. For the DVD video: Anneliese Varaldiev for her talent behind the lens and the microphone; Tom Carson for his construction expertise and high standards; Mary Jo Reutter for being "sun girl" at the straw bale and mud workshops; and for my hard-working and talented construction crew: Mark Steinkamp, Stefan Bell, Joe Yarkin, and Keely Meagan.

For Further Reading

There are many excellent and very well-known books on straw bale and green construction. Listed below are some publications that may be less familiar to you.

The Last Straw
The International Journal of Straw Bale and Natural Building
The techniques of building with straw are constantly changing and being revised. This quarterly publication is essential for keeping up with the latest developments.
Published by The Green Prairie Foundation
www.TheLastStraw.org

Environmental Building News
The Leading Newsletter on Environmentally Responsible Design and Construction
A web site and monthly publication featuring condensed and easy-to-understand information on all aspects of green building. It is particularly useful in researching the best green products and construction materials.
www.buildinggreen.com

The Earth Builders' Encyclopedia
Formerly a book, and now published as a CD-ROM, this covers the whole gamut of earth building from A to Z.
By Joesph M. Tibbets
Published by Southwest Solar Adobe School

Solar Living Sourcebook
By John Schaeffer
A complete catalogue and guide to products related to renewable energy and sustainable living. The book includes PV electrical systems, solar heating, wind power, water pumping, and much more.
Published by Gaiam Real Goods
Distributed by New Society Publishers

A Pattern Language: Towns, Buildings, Construction
By Christopher Alexander
Although not specifically about green building, this is a superb book on house design. It cuts through the seemingly overwhelming task of attaining good design and boils it down to a series of step-by-step decisions. If you thoughtfully work with the patterns presented, I believe that even the layman can design a beautiful and functional home.
Published by Oxford University Press

INDEX

DVD Video Information

Running Time: Main Program: 2 hours 42 minutes • Total running time including 2nd audio track, narrated slide show, and extra features: over 5 hours 45 minutes
Features: 2nd audio track with additional design and construction commentary • A 16-minute narrated slide show of construction details • Aspect Ratio: 4:3 • Digital Stereo Sound
Awards: 3 Telly Awards for Outstanding Multimedia DVD, Editing, and Graphics
Compatibility: Plays in all country regions with NTSC compatible DVD players and all personal computers capable of playing DVD videos

DVD Production Credits

Directed, Written, Photographed and Edited by
Ted Owens

A Production of
Syncronos Design Incorporated

Additional Photography and Narration by
Anneliese Varaldiev

Original Music Written and Performed by
Emily Dahmen

Production Coordinator
Mary Jo Reutter

Featuring

Tom Carson	**head construction consultant**
Mark Steinkamp	**construction assistant**
Stefan Bell	**straw bale and earth plaster expert**
Keely Meagan	**earth plaster finish coat expert**
Joe Yarkin	**photovoltaic and electrical wiring expert**
Al Owens	**main construction assistant**
Ted Owens	**designer and builder**

Produced and Published by Syncronos Design Inc.
DVD Copyright © 2005 by Ted Owens. All rights reserved.
Building With Awareness is a registered trademark of Ted Owens • DVD Made in USA